To DREAM as GOD DREAMS

Sermons of Community, Conversion, and Hope

Porter Taylor

morehouse

HARRISBURG • LONDON

Unless otherwise indicated, biblical quotations are from the New Revised Standard Version Bible, copyright 1989, Division of Christian Education of the National Council of the Churches of Christ in the United States of America. Used by permission. All rights reserved.

Scripture taken from The Message is copyright © by Eugene Peterson, 1993, 1994, 1995. Used by permission of NavPress Publishing Group.

Excerpt from *Learning to Live in the World: Earth Poems by William Stafford*, compilation copyright © 1994 by Jerry Watson and Laura Apol Obbink, reprinted by permission of Harcourt, Inc.

Published by

Morehouse Publishing, P.O. Box 1321, Harrisburg, PA 17105

Morehouse Publishing, The Tower Building, 11 York Road, London SE1 7NX

Morehouse Publishing is a Continuum imprint.

First published in 2000 by The Green Berry Press, 191 E. Broad St., Suite 322, Athens, GA 30601.

Cover art: "Mission Concepcion, San Antonio, Texas" courtesy of Richard Cummins/Superstock

Cover design by Wesley Hoke.

Library of Congress Cataloging-in-Publication Data

Taylor, G. Porter.

To dream as God dreams : sermons of community, conversion, and hope / Porter Taylor.

p. cm.

ISBN 0-8192-2165-1 (pbk.)

1. Episcopal Church—Sermons. 2. Sermons, American—21st century. I. Title.

BX5937.T29T6 2005

252'.03—dc22

2004019152

Printed in the United States of America

04 05 06 07 08 09   10 9 8 7 6 5 4 3 2 1

To Jo
Who shows me, again and again,
that God is in the simple details
of our common, wonderful lives

Contents

The Deepest Longing: Sermons for Transitions

Introduction

At the end of every week, there is a collective *angst* over the world as priests and ministers accept that Sunday is drawing near and they can no longer put off the hard work of writing a sermon. We sit at our desks and ask ourselves, "What in the world do I have to say?" Between that moment and when we stand in the pulpit Sunday morning, the answer comes: "I have my story, the people's story, and the Sacred Story." Like a verbal tapestry, we try to weave the three together so that each defines the other.

These sermons span eight years and come from a variety of settings. Most of them were preached during the Holy Eucharist on Sunday morning either at St. Paul's Episcopal Church in Franklin, Tennessee, or St. Gregory the Great Episcopal Church in Athens, Georgia. This collection also includes sermons at funerals and ordinations. Each is an attempt to gaze at our lives and our world through the lens of Scripture. I often speak of my personal history because it's the only way I know to embrace the Scripture. I have never doubted the reality of the biblical history, but I want to know what it means for me in this moment in this place. I have changed people's names whenever the circumstances might be embarrassing. If any references remain which should have been removed, I apologize.

Reading sermons is sort of like reading scripts for plays. They give directions for what is supposed to happen, but they cannot and do not duplicate the moment of preaching because preaching is at its core interactive. Something happens in the midst of the preacher and the people. I, therefore, write sermons as points of departure and not as polished texts. I have tried to remove most of the unorthodox punctuation that I use to signal pauses or places for emphasis. I have, however, left the syntax as it is, even though the cadences are for oral delivery more than they are to be read.

I am grateful to those parishioners who conceived of this project and did the hard work to make it possible, especially Al Hester and Sandra Hudson. I also want to thank all of the people in both churches who shared their hopes and dreams, their pains and sorrows, and their doubts and faith with me.

At their best, sermons are conversations about things that matter. As parishioners have been genuine with me, they have allowed me to be genuine with them. Most of all, I am grateful to my family: Arthur, my son; Marie, my daughter; and Jo, my wife. Through their love for me and their reception of my love for them, I have learned of God's love for all of us.

Building Up the Body of Christ
Sermons of Community

Finding Our Storm Home

 ISAIAH 25:1–9; PSALM 23; PHILIPPIANS 4:4–13; MATTHEW 22:1–14

I shall dwell in the house of the LORD my whole life long.
PSALM 23:6

Our world is a world of change. A world that seems to spin faster and faster.

Places change. When I left Nashville there was no Cool Springs Mall. The first time I drove down I-65, for a minute I didn't know where I was.

Maybe to keep up with these changes, people move. Every ten years, fifty percent of the American population moves. My son is nine years old and he has lived in six different houses.

Although we no longer tend flocks and live by the seasons, we have again become a nomadic people. In a world of drastic change—where is home?

Even if you are living in the house in which you grew up, this is still the main question. For home is where you belong; where you are accepted; where those deepest longings of your heart can be met. Home is not just a place; it's a condition. And you can have lived in Franklin, Tennessee, all your life and still not feel at home.

When will we find our home? All three readings as well as the psalm address this problem. And this is the answer they give: So long as we are on this earth, this fragile island, our only home is the presence of God. No house or family will fully satisfy our deepest longing. There is a hole in our heart only God can fill.

But we are given a promise of a real home, a banquet, a wedding feast in the kingdom. In the kingdom, God will:

> *Swallow up death;*
> *The Lord will wipe away our tears;* (Isaiah 25:8)
> *We will not be in want;*
> *God will anoint our heads with oil;*
> *Our cup will run over;*
> *We will have a home to dwell in forever.* (Psalm 23)

But, you know, Christianity is always a paradox. Thomas Merton says, "In one sense we are always traveling. . . . In another sense we have already arrived."[1]

Like Isaiah, we long for a shelter; we look forward to a feast. Isaiah lived in the southern kingdom, and Judah had just been overtaken by the Assyrians. Isaiah longed for the day when the Hebrew people would again be free. And Paul writes his letter to the Philippians from prison. He knows what it is to be in need, to have little, and, of course, to be persecuted for one's faith.

For Isaiah, for the psalmist, for Paul—where is home? It's both in the future and it's right here.

As I thought about this sermon, I kept thinking of a story that Garrison Keillor told. He talks about going to school during the fierce winters of Minnesota:

> Mr. Detman, our principal had his own winter fear: that a blizzard would sweep in and school buses be marooned on the roads and children perish. So he announced that each pupil that lived in the country would be assigned a storm home in town. If a blizzard struck during school, we'd go to our storm home.
>
> Mine was the Kloeckls, an old couple who lived in a little green cottage by the lake. It looked like the home of the kindly old couple that the children lost in the forest suddenly come upon in a clearing and know they are lucky to be in a story with a happy ending.
>
> I imagined the Kloeckls had personally chosen me as their storm child because they liked me. "Him!" they had told Mr. Detman. "In the event of a blizzard, we want that boy. The skinny one with the thick glasses!"[2]

Isaiah lived during a storm, and so did Paul, and so did the psalmist, and so did Matthew, and so do you and I. Outside, the clouds

1. Thomas Merton, "Meditatio Pauperis in Solitudine," in *A Thomas Merton Reader* (Garden City, NY: Image Books, 1974), 513.
2. Garrison Keillor, *Lake Wobegon Days* (New York: Viking, 1985), 248–49.

are always gathering, and as much as we try to get things fixed just the way we want them, nothing stays in place. Our lives change. And like the boy in Garrison Keillor's story, we are afraid of being trapped in some school building far away from home.

At some deep level, I believe that's where we are. We say to ourselves, *"Things weren't supposed to turn out this way."* People weren't supposed to suffer or die or get divorced or move away. Our cities weren't supposed to become such violent places. People we respected weren't supposed to make mistakes in their personal lives and shock and disappoint us.

We don't want to hear about all the troubled places. We feel like we are in the seventh grade, and it's beginning to snow. The other children are on their way home because they live close, but our home is far away, and no buses are running.

And then maybe we remember something from Paul:

> *The LORD is near. Do not worry about anything. . . . And the peace of God, which surpasses all understanding, will guard your hearts and your minds in Christ Jesus.*
> (Philippians 4:5–7)

Every time it starts snowing in our hearts and we feel trapped in some distant place—remember we have been promised a Storm Home: And that is in the arms of Jesus Christ.

The Saints of God
A Sermon for All Saints' Day

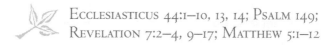

ECCLESIASTICUS 44:1–10, 13, 14; PSALM 149;
REVELATION 7:2–4, 9–17; MATTHEW 5:1–12

Let us now sing the praises of famous men,
our ancestors in their generations.
ECCLESIASTICUS 44:1

This week I saw an amazing film: *Pleasantville*. It's about a teenage set of twins who are somehow transported from 1998 into a 1950s television program called *Pleasantville*. *Pleasantville* is much like *Leave it to Beaver*—it's a one-dimensional world. Everything is always pleasant. No one ever ages, and no one has any idea what lies outside Pleasantville.

The people of Pleasantville deny the reality of time. They deny the communion of the present with the past and the future. In Pleasantville, all roads go in a circle. They don't come from somewhere and go somewhere else.

Now this may seem a little far-fetched to us. After all, it's only a movie. But *Pleasantville* points to a particularly American phenomenon. We think of ourselves as ahistorical, isolated individuals. Ralph Waldo Emerson described himself as "an endless seeker with no past at my back."

We have this illusion that we were born *ex nihilo*—out of nothing. Henry Ford said, in his typical American way, "All history is bunk." We have the illusion that we owe nothing to the past and nothing to the future, but we only focus on now. It's just ME living in my digital moment. So I don't have to pay any attention to those who came before; I don't care about those who come after me. In the film, all the books in the library are blank because there is no memory. Because nothing new ever happens—no new generation is ever born.

Well, something happens in the film *Pleasantville*. And, we pray, something happens to us. In the film, the brother and sister bring life into this static world. As they touch other people—as they encounter

5

people and broaden their perspective, slowly the world and the people change from black and white into color.

Bud, the brother from our time, says to the mayor of Pleasantville:

> The people now in color are not any "different." They
> just see something inside that you don't see.

Now what has all this to do with the feast of All Saints?

As Bud says—saints are not any different. "They just see something inside that we don't see." Saints are ordinary people who see the face of Christ in other people's faces. Saints are Christ-bearers, or what Presbyterian pastor and writer Frederick Buechner calls "life-givers": men and women who are so filled with Christ's love that they are radiant. The light within them spreads all about them. When we come into their presence, saints change us from black and white into color.

They help us feel alive. They help us incarnate as the people we were created to be. They remind us that being fully human means that the divine Holy Spirit resides in our mortal bodies, that God is to be found in our flawed lives.

We celebrate saints not so much for what they do, but for who they are. On this All Saints' Day we celebrate the fact that we do not live in Pleasantville. Our roads do not go in a circle. We are part of a great history. We hold hands with those who have come before and those who will follow us.

Therefore, All Saints' Day is a celebration of our living in time. First, we celebrate those who have gone before us: the famous and the unfamous, the people who have touched our lives and brought us from death into life. The people who have loved us along the way.

Sometimes when I look up from the altar, the faces of the congregation are blended into the faces on the mural at the rear of our church. For a moment I see Martha and Cecelia and Gregory and John with us. But it's no illusion. It's just that those are the moments I see clearly.

Remember the film, *Places of the Heart?* The film ends at a Protestant church. The congregation is taking communion, and those who have died in the film sit with the living. Everyone feeds from the body and blood of Christ. As we say in the eucharistic prayer: "Now with Angels and

Archangels and all the company of heaven." All those we have loved and who have died are here in a holy communion, the famous and the unfamous.

Everyone is in the great parade: People like Abraham and Sarah, Joseph and Mary, Paul and Mary Magdalene, Augustine, St. Francis, Thomas Cranmer, William White, William Stringfellow, William Temple. And people who are not in any book. People like Julia Capps who taught me eleventh-grade English, and Finley Cooper, a priest in charge of our EYC group. And Jayne Haynes, and my grandmother, and my father and my uncle.

I wouldn't be here without them, and I wouldn't get to tomorrow without their help. The mystery is that the past is alive in us. Over and over again, I hear my father's voice coming out of my mouth. I say to my kids, "What were you thinking when you did that?" And when I look at them, they are me, and time falls back upon itself.

So we celebrate the past, but we also prepare for those who come after us. When we baptize someone, we baptize them into the body of Christ. As they are baptized, we will be handing on to them what we have received from our ancestors. We will say to them: You are now part of the parade; you are a Christ-bearer to the world. We are commissioning them to carry the light into the world after we are gone.

The Navajos have a saying that every time we make a decision we should consider its effect on the seventh generation. For you and I do not live for ourselves; the future depends on us.

When we celebrate all the saints, we also celebrate those to come. We celebrate those to be baptized as well as their children and their children's children. We pass the faith to them so they can pass it on in their turn.

And finally, the hardest is us—right now in this moment.

In the novel, *The Power and the Glory*, Graham Greene writes about a priest who has led a very sinful life. On his deathbed, he has a realization:

> He felt only an immense disappointment because he had to go to God empty-handed, with nothing done at all. He felt like someone who has missed happiness by seconds at an appointed place. He now knew that at the end there was only one thing that counted—to be a saint.

We are not called merely to honor saints or prepare for future saints; we are called to be saints. As absurd as it may seem, God has picked such unlikely people as you and me to receive the love of Christ and to take that love into the world.

We don't have to go to Calcutta. We don't have to sell all our possessions and give them away to the poor. We don't need a march on Washington. We need to receive the love God is always giving us.

For the chalice here today at St. Gregory the Great is the cup of salvation, and the bread baked by the women in this parish really is the bread of heaven. God is calling us to let go of our fears; to let go of our illusion that we are isolated from the past and future and isolated from one another; to receive God's grace and to carry that love into the world. For the truth is, it doesn't take much to transform the world. It only takes a little love, a little courage, and touch. It takes an encounter.

Who else is going to change the world? Who else is going to turn a black-and-white world into color? Drugs—racism—the poor without hope—schools filled with violence—a world where a person like Matthew Shepard is beaten to death because he is gay. Who else is going to bring the redemptive love of Jesus Christ into the world?

We honor the past; we sow seeds for the future. However, we pray for God to use us. For the saints of God are just folk like me, and I mean to be one, too.

Roots and Wings

Preached on Epiphany

 ISAIAH 42:1–9; PSALM 89:1–29 OR 89:20–29; ACTS 10:34–38; MATTHEW 3:13–17

> *And when Jesus had been baptized, just as he came up from the water, suddenly the heavens were opened to him and he saw the Spirit of God descending like a dove and alighting on him. And a voice from heaven said, "This is my Son, the Beloved, with whom I am well pleased."*
> MATTHEW 3:16–17

Parents can give two gifts to their children: Roots and Wings.

Roots mean you know who you are. You know where you come from. If we know our roots, then we know that we are part of something bigger than our lifespan. Now, if you are from the South, this may not be a problem for you. We are big on roots. When I go to my mother's family's reunion, the Richardson clan, every "hello" lasts 10 minutes, because it begins with "Now, let's see—your momma's uncle married the first cousin of my granddaddy's brother." Even while you are nodding, this crowd of people is gathering to supply names and dates and stories about Uncle Joe Frank who came up from Moncks Corner to Columbia in '25.

We all need roots; even people from strange places like New York need roots. We need to know that we are not defined by this moment or that our identity goes deeper than our present circumstances: Who we are is not about what we own or what we do or what others think of us.

But the need for roots is deeper than being connected to our parents. We yearn for a holy communion—to be connected to those who have gone before, and to our Lord Jesus Christ, and, through him, to one another.

Today we celebrate Jesus' baptism, and God shows us what it is to give God's Son and, therefore, all of us real roots and real wings. God says to those around Jesus:

This is my Son, the Beloved, with whom I am well
pleased.

And God says that to every person baptized: "You are my child;
you belong to me; you are the Beloved and I am pleased with you."
Those are the words that tell us who we are. I am not just Joe Frank's
second cousin four times removed. I am an ordinary sinner who is loved
by God, because God is love. And so are you.

The core of the Christian life is receiving that amazing gift. But
how often we cannot open our hands. How often we make love into a
commodity we have to buy or that is beyond our means.

I have a friend who went through a period of self-doubt—even
self-loathing. Every time she looked at someone, all she saw was criti-
cism. And so she began to withdraw more and more. One evening, she
was walking after a meeting, and she happened to run into an old friend
she hadn't seen for a while. The friend, instinctively, intuitively, reached
out her hand and caressed the woman's face and said, "You are so beautiful." And that simple gesture changed everything. It reminded her that
she was connected. She had roots. She was loved.

But roots are useless without wings. Wings mean we can do things
that have never been done before. Wings mean that the past feeds us but
does not limit us. So the passage from Isaiah ends with

See, the former things [God sent] have come to pass,
and new things I now declare.

Now, let's not confuse wings with self-expression. The "new
things" are not meaningless assertions of one's own freedom. Our wings
are not the power to alter our appearance or to break every rule our parents made. Someone gave me a pad of Post-it® notes that says: "No
rules—no boundaries—no problem." Or, as Outback Steakhouse® says,
"No rules—just right." That's not wings. That's a denial of being the
beloved. That's a refusal to embrace one's roots.

No, to have wings is to have courage to live out our covenant
with God.

Remember the film *Dead Poets Society?* One of the students, named
Neil, wants to be an actor, but his father is insistent. No, he is fanatical,

about his son's becoming a doctor. Neil signs up for a play against his father's will. There is an ugly confrontation, and the father says: "You tell them you are quitting. I've made enough sacrifices to get you in this school. You are not letting me down." Well, the son makes the ultimate sacrifice and takes his life, because the father cannot love his son for who he is. He cannot give his son roots or wings, and Neil falls into the earth of his grave.

Parents need to give the blessing and set their children free to flourish. Knowing who we are enables us to focus on the world outside our selves and discover a communion.

What is true for our biological parents is true for God. God pronounces God's blessing at the River Jordan and Jesus sets about his ministry. Once we know we are God's beloved, then God sends us into the world to spread the good news. God says to us what he says to Isaiah:

> *I have given you as a covenant to the people, a light to the nations, to open the eyes that are blind, to bring out the prisoners from the dungeon, from the prison those who sit in darkness.*

Our wings are not just to find the right profession or vocation but to do works of mercy and justice in the world, finally to have the courage to love one another as Christ has loved us. To forgive one another—to be just to one another. To stop the cycle of violence in which so many of our brothers and sisters are trapped. To do justice.

And we do that by embracing our belovedness and living that blessing out in the world. We have been given a great gift, and God is calling on us to use it. Our wings are what enable us to do something new; to see the world in new ways; to see how our world perpetuates cycles of injustice. And to set people free.

A reporter was in Sarajevo during the worst of the violence, and one day he was walking down the street and a bomb went off. A young boy was critically injured and the reporter ran over to help. A man was bent over the boy and asked the reporter, "Please help me get my child to the hospital." So the reporter flagged a taxi and the three of them raced off.

As they traveled, the man said over and over again: "I am afraid my child is dying."

When they got to the hospital, the medics took the boy into ICU and the reporter told the man, "I hope your son is all right."

"Oh," replied the man, "I'm not his father."

"But you came all this way," the reporter said.

The man looked at him and said, "Aren't they all our children?"

Once we know we are the Beloved and that we are indeed God's children, then we can have wings to turn to all our brothers and sisters and know that they are God's children, too.

Forgiving Our "Weediness"

 WISDOM 12:13, 16–19; PSALM 86 OR 86:11–17;
ROMANS 8:18–25; MATTHEW 13:24–30, 36–43

> *Let both [the wheat and the weeds] grow together until the*
> *harvest.*
> MATTHEW 13:30

Let's start with a quote from the theologian Reinhold Niebuhr:

> *Nothing that is worth doing can be achieved in our lifetime—there-*
> *fore we must be saved by hope; Nothing which is true or beautiful*
> *or good makes complete sense in the immediate context of history—*
> *therefore we must be saved by faith; Nothing we do, however virtu-*
> *ous, can be accomplished alone—therefore we must be saved by love.*
> *No virtuous act is quite as virtuous from the standpoint of our*
> *friend or foe as it is from our standpoint—therefore we must be*
> *saved by the final form of love which is forgiveness.*[3]

I confess I do not have a green thumb. In fact I believe that I am
botanically illiterate. If it's green, it all looks the same to me. As a result,
I am a disaster as a weeder, at least until the plants come into bloom.
When they are all green, I am just as likely to pull up a zinnia or tomato
plant as a weed.

But, even though it irritates some people in my household, the
stakes really aren't too high. I don't pull up anything very expensive—
no gardenia bushes or magnolia trees. Besides, we have a long growing
season and can always start over with new plants.

So, at first hearing, this parable doesn't have much of a bite. Who
cares about wheat and weeds anyway? But Jesus isn't really talking about
plants. He's talking about people, and the stakes are much higher.

As soon as we know that the division is between good and bad

---

3. Reinhold Niebuhr, *The Irony of American History* (New York: Charles Scribner's Sons,
1952), 63.

people, we want to know who are the weeds and who are the wheat. However, it never is that simple, is it? The wheat and weeds are all tangled up. It's hard to tell who is who. Maybe we like action movies like *Rambo, Die Hard, Terminator, Mission: Impossible,* and *The Bourne Identity* because good and evil are so clear. The film begins, and our guy is goodness incarnate and the villain is evil incarnate. We can adore our side and despise the other side with abandon. We munch our popcorn and know that in two hours the villains will be eliminated or weeded out. There's part of us that wishes all of life were melodrama, but it never is.

Instead, life is always this mix of weeds and wheat—both in our society and in ourselves. When Jesus describes the weeds, he isn't talking about your average Middle East weeds. He actually is describing a plant called *darnel*. This is a weed that looks exactly like wheat until both are fully grown. Only as they bear fruit can one discern the difference between them. There is a difference in the fruit; the grain of wheat nourishes us, but the grain of *darnel* can poison us.

Because we know how dangerous *darnel* is, we want to weed it out early. But we need to heed Jesus' warning. He tells us: *You cannot see clearly enough. If you try to do the weeding, you will put up wheat with weeds, because God isn't finished with God's creation. It's too early to tell who is the wheat and who is the weed.* What we may think is wheat may be weeds and what looks like weeds may be wheat. Unfortunately, we humans are an impatient lot. We want to get on with the weeding. We don't like waiting around to see what's what. We want clear distinctions. So we try weeding ourselves.

Our history is littered with human attempts at weeding, and they are all disasters: there's the Inquisition and the Salem witch trials. There's the McCarthy era and the John Birch Society.

Hitler was a weeder and so are Slobadon Milosevic, Osama bin Laden, and Saddam Hussein. Every attempt to weed out evil by removing people ends up being evil itself. Let's remember that no one—except perhaps a sociopath—intentionally does evil acts. We all believe that we are divine weeders, but human beings are infinitely capable of self-deception. It's why the slogan of so many child abusers is "for your own good."

So what does our Lord suggest? Are we to simply say, "Weed, wheat—it's all the same to me?" Are we just to ignore the noxious plants around us and pretend all is well?

No, what Jesus says is, *"Let both of them grow together until the harvest; and at harvest time I will tell the reapers, Collect the weeds first and bind them in bundles to be burned."* We are to focus on the wheat. We are to water the whole field, and give it all it needs. When we see something that looks like a weed, give it the benefit of the doubt. Nourish it; water it; wish it well; hope it grows into wheat and not weeds. And know that in God's good time, God will harvest and divide the good from the bad. We do not live in a relative world. Wheat feeds us and weeds kill us. But God will pull up the weeds, and God will set them on fire.

Last year I went to my thirtieth high school reunion. What a strange experience that was! Some people hadn't changed at all. My twin sister's best friend still looked and acted the same. But some people were total surprises. Frank, the president of the Latin Club and a real nerd, has fought cocaine addiction for 20 years. But Margaret, a sort of wispy, quiet girl who sat in the corner and never was even on the fringe of the "in" crowd, is a famous priest in the church and a fire-breathing feminist. Sharon, the homecoming queen, lives in a condo on Miami Beach and runs a beauty salon.

Thirty years ago I thought I knew so much, but I knew nothing. I couldn't tell who would grow up to be wheat or weeds. And you know what? I still couldn't tell that at the reunion because it isn't time for the harvest. Who knows what God has in store for Frank or Margaret or Sharon? Or for you or me? We are always in the green time, the in-between time, the time when the plants are up but we don't know what they are going to be. We don't know what fruit they will yield.

So we need to be patient with one another. In fact the Greek word for "let" is *aphete*. *Aphete* is also the root for the word "forgive"—as in *"Forgive us our trespasses as we forgive those who trespass against us."* We might say, "forgive our weeds as we forgive the weediness of others." Because both weeds and wheat are inside each of us. Therefore, we need to pray for God to nourish our wheat and root out our weeds. We can spend too much time on our weeds and not enough time on our wheat. I mean, while it does help to be honest about our problems and our sins, growth comes from watering the wheat.

After awhile, it doesn't help to focus on the weeds; it's the wheat that matters. It's the wheat that will feed us. It's the wheat that will be the bread of life. I mean that in terms of our community and in terms of ourselves. In terms of our community—let's assert what we are for and not just what we are against. You cannot be nourished by being negative. Our souls are never fed by only saying, "I am against that," or "I am against those people."

The question is, "What are you for? Where have you found the wheat? What is it in your life that will make the bread of life?"

And in terms of ourselves—if we are to grow and have what Jesus calls "abundant life" we must embrace the parts of our lives that feed us and not always focus on what is wrong. We must embrace life and not merely whine over the death that surrounds us. I have said before that the best class I ever took was a year-long class on Dante. This was a graduate seminar, so each student made a presentation. There was one student who was totally out of it. He did not have a clue. He was to report on canto 30 of the *Paradiso*, perhaps the most beautiful poetry in any language. He talked for a while, and then he answered some questions.

Now, understand that the professor, Arthur Evans, was a very devout Catholic. And he was a true mystic, deeply immersed in the spiritual masters. Someone asked the student about the place of the Blessed Virgin Mary in the canto, and he said, "To tell the truth, I couldn't see why Dante made such a big deal over Mary. I mean she was just another woman as far as I was concerned." My mouth dropped. I had a hard time imagining that anyone could think such a thing, much less say it. And I looked to Arthur Evans. Surely he would set this person straight. Surely he would separate the wheat from the weeds, pull this person out and toss him into the fire. But Arthur looked at the student and simply said, "That's a thought I've never come across. Why don't you tell us about your religious background?"

We are all so weed-ridden, any one of us on any day can start tossing someone else out because we've exposed our weeds. But instead, let us nourish the wheat. Let us help one another grow so that our Lord can use our wheat to make the bread of life.

Eating Doritos® at the Rejects Prom

EZEKIEL 34:11–17; I CORINTHIANS 15:20–28;
MATTHEW 25:31–46

*All the nations will be gathered before him, and he will separate
people one from another as a shepherd separates the sheep from
the goats.*
MATTHEW 25:32

Isn't it frustrating when the world doesn't conform to our private sense of
order? The Scripture, if we take it seriously, is especially frustrating. We want
it to say what we want it to say, but sometimes the text doesn't cooperate.

I have read this passage from Matthew a million times. In fact,
when I saw it in the lectionary, I thought to myself, "No problem. I
already know what this one means." This passage is so well known that
a homeless shelter in Nashville is named "Matthew 25" because we all
know that the point of the passage is to shelter the homeless and feed
the hungry and clothe the naked.

Jesus is telling us to share what we have with those who have nothing. Jesus says if we want to serve him, we are to serve what he calls the
"little ones"—the poor, the disadvantaged, the oppressed—the people
in our world we overlook as we go about our busy and important lives.
He is warning us against middle-class complacency and selfishness—
right? Well, "yes" and "no."

Jesus does call us to do love by helping the "little ones." We are to
treat them the way we would treat Jesus. In fact we are to look for Jesus
in them.

But the text is more slippery than we think. I am all set to get into
a sort of righteously indignant rant about our selfishness and greed and
neglect of those less fortunate than we. Unfortunately, the text will not
cooperate; it doesn't say that. I wish we could sort of gloss over the
words that don't fit, but we actually can't. Let's look at the text:

> *When the Son of Man comes in his glory, and all the angels with him,
> then he will sit on the throne of his glory. All the nations will be*

17

gathered before him, and he will separate people one from another
as a shepherd separates the sheep from the goats.

The problem is "all the nations." We assume that means everyone and then go on to read the passage in terms of God judging all people by this criterion. Here's the rub. First of all, even if we read it this way, it's a problem because it discounts grace. If we look at God in this light, then God becomes a bean counter—a sort of divine Santa Claus who is checking his list twice. If we are too selfish, too greedy, or simply too unaware to notice those "little ones" of the world, then it's Good Night Gracie for us. We are off to the place where it never freezes over.

But the biggest problem is with the word "nations." It doesn't mean "everyone." The word for "everyone" is *pantes*. Matthew uses the word *ethne*; *ethne* is a technical term designating non-Jewish individuals. It is a synonym for *goyim*: those outside the Chosen People.

So whether we like it or not, Jesus isn't saying "Everyone will be gathered before him, and he will separate people one from another." Instead, Jesus is talking to the Jews—those who believe in Him—and he is saying this:

You know that you belong to me and that you will be with me always,
even to the end of the age; but do not think that I have abandoned
the rest. Even they will have a door into the kingdom; for if they
have fed the hungry and clothed the naked and given shelter to the
homeless, they have seen my face and they have served me.

Oh. That's not what we came to hear, is it? If we have to throw away our "indignant rant," what does this text have to say to us? Well, after we get over our disappointment, it actually says a lot.

First it reminds us that God is always bigger than us. As we hear in Isaiah: God's ways are not our ways. This is the last Sunday of the church year. Next Sunday begins Advent. In the church calendar, we call this Christ the King Sunday.

Historically, Jesus plays three roles: priest, prophet, and king. The priest is the Good Shepherd—the Jesus who consoles the broken-hearted and binds up our wounds. The prophet is Jesus who kicks out the money changers or the "Woe to you" Jesus in Luke's Beatitudes. But the

King is the Jesus who embraces all sorts and conditions of people. The King is the Cosmic Christ who, despite Pilate's delusions of grandeur, is the ruler of the world.

For God so loved the world, the whole world, every man and woman in every place, God so loved them all—Gentile and Jew— that God sent God's only Son. So the first reminder here is that we do not have a monopoly on salvation. God's grace is always bigger than we think.

Thursday is Thanksgiving, and in many places there is a tradition of leaving an empty chair at the table. The chair was for the unexpected guest, the stranger who may be an angel. Of course, this is close to the Jewish custom at the Passover Seder of leaving a chair for Elijah to join them. In like manner, let us never believe we have taken every chair in the kingdom. Let's not think that God loves us best or that for us to feel really good about our own salvation we have vicariously to enjoy the notion of all those other people frying in the eternal fire. When the Son of Man comes in all His glory, he will call all those other people whom we have already written off—those people that we know are completely wrong about their beliefs—and he will look at how they have lived their lives.

Now, I have no idea how God's mind works, but because of what I know about God's grace, I have a hard time imagining Gandhi being condemned to eternal damnation or countless other folks from other traditions that we know nothing about. So part of this Christ the King Sunday is to marvel at God's generosity and grace and to realize that our notions of God's ways are always too small.

Second, if this is what God demands of pagans, what must God expect of us—the people who have been taught the Scriptures and nourished by the sacraments? Our motive is not to win God's love; God already loves us. Our motive is not to earn eternal life; it's a gift freely given from God's grace. But our motive must be to please God by helping God bring in the kingdom of mercy and grace and justice and peace. It's like showing love to your spouse or child or, on good days, your brother or sister or parent. It's not an obligation. It's a natural response. We love others because God loves us. Love is not something we feel; it's something we do.

Do you know the best part of Thanksgiving for me? It's not the meal itself although that is nice. It's the leftovers. It's forgetting about cholesterol and making a turkey sandwich with plenty of mayonnaise. It's like the party after the party when there is no pressure to make the meal into some kind of Norman Rockwell painting.

But for too many people in our opulent country, there are no leftovers. Yes, they may be able to have a turkey dinner on November 25, but then what? There are no leftovers in the fridge. There is no party after the party. There is just the return to their life where they are left by the side of the road and stepped over.

As we think of what God demands of those *ethnes*, let us think about what God demands of us. Let us think about how we can leave empty chairs not just at this table but at our kitchen tables. Let us think about how we can construct a world where no one is left by and stepped over.

To think about this, let's compare two junk food commercials: The Ruffles® ad has one person gorging himself while another stares at him. The one without Ruffles® asks for a chip, but the man says, "If I gave one to you, I would have to give one to everybody." The slogan comes on: "So good you'd better get your own bag." Well, the Doritos® slogan is more in line with what God expects of us: "Crunch all you want. . . . We'll make more!" Let's not protect our bags. Let's open them up knowing that God has plenty of grace for everyone.

Finally, and the best news for me, Christ the King is everywhere. *"Just as you did [works of mercy] to the least of these who are members of my family, you did it to me."* It's astonishing how often we forget the incarnation. The Word became flesh and dwells among us. We keep fixating our gaze up and forgetting to look at one another.

Do you want to serve Christ? Serve other people. Do not wait until after you die to see your Lord. Open your eyes and look into the face of those who have no protection. Look for the eyes of Christ in that person's eyes. St. Francis had his greatest experience of the presence of Jesus when he kissed a leper. It wasn't in St. Peter's in Rome. It wasn't saying his prayers. It wasn't doing "holy acts." It was when he overcame his disgust for the ugliness of the leper's sores and when he embraced the man walking down the path and kissed him on the cheek that Francis saw Jesus.

Do you want to touch the risen Christ? Then do not wait; He is everywhere. Jesus is always looking for you—trying to catch your glance—trying to embrace you. And all we see is what our culture tells us to see.

One night when we lived in Nashville, we were at the Opryland hotel and I overheard a woman who was obviously a tourist ask her friend, "Who is that man over there?"

"Oh," her friend replied. "It's no one famous. Just a nobody."

No one is nobody. No one. If we but had eyes to see, we'd see the face of Jesus Christ. So we are all called to do works of mercy. We are to remember that we are all working for the kingdom. And let us not lose hope.

I came across an interesting image in Tony Campolo's book *The Kingdom of God Is a Party*. He writes that a Lutheran minister got tired of so many high school kids getting depressed over not having a date for the prom, so his church started a party called "The Rejects Prom." It was for people without dates and was held the same night as the prom. The amazing thing is that the Rejects Prom became so successful that it got press coverage, and soon corporations were giving door prizes. After a year or so, the Rejects Prom became more popular than the prom itself.

Maybe that's an image we ought to hold in mind: We may think that because we are here, we have a date to the prom. But don't forget, there's a prom for those we think are rejects. And the amazing thing is their prom is the same as ours.

Love from the Center

 EZEKIEL 33:(1–6) 7–11; PSALM 119:33–48 OR
119:33–40; ROMANS 12:9–21; MATTHEW 18:15–20

Let love be genuine; hate what is evil, hold fast to what is good.
ROMANS 12:9

In today's epistle, Paul is trying to teach the Romans how to be the church—the true church, the place of Holy Communion. But it's not easy. Everyone is squabbling. The Jewish Christians start calling the Gentile Christians names. So now they refuse to worship with one another. Then the Roman Christians won't talk to the non-Roman Christians; so they end up sitting on opposite sides of the aisles. At coffee hour, groups form. Little circles of people gather like wagon trains to protect themselves from those "other people." The conversations are spiced with words like "heretic" and "apostate." Or "stupid Roman" or "radical Gentile."

The Roman church reminds Paul of ice on a frozen lake as it begins to crack and divide. Chunks of ice drift apart in the dark water, as the once-solid lake becomes a sea of islands of ice. It's like Humpty Dumpty. How in the world can it be put together again?

Well, Paul doesn't mention some of the worst tactics the church has used in the past 2,000 years: No burning at the stake. No silencing people you disagree with. No dividing into smaller and smaller sects. No outlawing of certain books. No sacking of monasteries. No locking people in the Tower.

In fact, in the face of this list, Paul's suggestions look a little wimpy. He gives some rules about behavior—*contribute to the needs of the saints; extend hospitality to strangers; do not repay anyone evil for evil. If your enemies are hungry, feed them.* These are daunting, but at least they are clear. Often we need to begin with specific acts. Certainly there is a correlation between our actions and our inner state.

It is true that our hearts will often follow our feet. If we keep doing the right thing, eventually we will feel the right emotion. But there is limitation to that method. We can get into a "works righteousness" mentality that keeps us from the real work of conversion. We do just acts in order to prove how wonderful we are and to preserve our righteous self-image. Therefore, this morning I want to focus on the interior side—the conversion of the heart.

The first thing Paul suggests is:

> *Let love be genuine . . . be ardent in spirit.* (Romans 12:9)

Perhaps Paul lists *"let love be genuine"* first for a reason. Perhaps if we can discover that place of genuineness, then all else will follow.

What does it mean to *let love be genuine?* Eugene Peterson translates this phrase in an interesting way:

> *Love from the center of who you are; don't fake it.*

To love from the center, to love genuinely, is to know who you are at your center. Most of the time we don't know. We usually either suffer from an overly inflated ego or an inadequate sense of who we are. We think we are so wonderful that everyone should be just like us— sort of like Rex Harrison when he sings in *My Fair Lady*, "Why can't a woman be like a man? Why can't a woman be more like me?"

When our ego is so inflated, we constantly are shoring it up. We are always needing others to certify how wonderful we are, and if they do not, then we demonize them. Or, on the other hand, when our ego is deflated, then we look for someone to worship, someone to tell us who we are.

Both of these are disingenuous love, and they always lead to either pushing or pulling others.

Either I am pushing you away, making you wrong so I can be right, or I am pulling you toward me by clutching onto you for an identity. Disingenuous love makes others into idols to worship or demons to despise until we discover our center. Until we find how to love genuinely, we can never find community.

Being around people who are in the grip of disingenuous love is so exhausting because everything centers on them. You cannot have a discussion without it becoming a referendum on their self-worth. So every conflict has very high stakes. We aren't just talking about whether to order red or black prayer books; we are talking about whether you affirm who I am.

Love from the center of who you are. Who we all are is this wonderful paradox: we are all sinners; we are all imperfect; we are all capable of causing one another pain. Yet, we are all children of God; we all
have Jesus Christ within us. We are all God's Beloved. Both things are
true.

Once we embrace that, then we can relax, because we can be merely
human, not angelic—not demonic—but just from the very earth. When
we know who we are, then we know that God is in control, and God
will do what God will do. We don't have to be in charge or go around
looking for some savior to be in charge. Instead, we can look to see what
God is doing in this place and accept it and try to participate in it.

Think about Jesus and the way he encountered other people, always
with open arms:

What do you want me to do for you?

Not, *Are you ready to fall down and worship me—or, Can you prove that
you are worthy of my presence?* But, *What do you want me to do for you?*

In other words—*Speak from your center and I will speak and act from
mine. We will see what happens among us—between us.*

Jesus Christ offers us the peace the world cannot give and the world
cannot take away. It's the peace of knowing that it's okay that we are sinners and screw up, because he will always love us and be with us and be
inside us. Once we know that deep in our hearts and souls, then we
relax. We don't need others to constantly affirm us. We don't need
someone else to look bad so we will look good. And an amazing thing
happens. We begin to see that everyone else is just like us, merely
human, merely sinners who are redeemed by the love of Christ.

Then it's all okay. Then the open arms that embrace one another
can also become the open arms on the cross, because the world no
longer has to conform to my idea of the way life should be. The world
can be what it is.

I heard someone say, *"The best ally of God is reality."* In order to
advance on the spiritual path, in order to grow in the divine school of
love, we must become fully alive in this world—as it is—because it is
the only world we have. The Word became flesh and dwells among us,
right here in the very world in which we live.

In *The Great Divorce*, C. S. Lewis says that hell is a vast, gray city only inhabited at its outer edges. In the middle are rows and rows of empty houses. Empty because everyone who lived in them quarreled with their neighbors and moved away. Then they quarreled and moved and quarreled and moved.

When I read that, I thought of our contemporary cities—abandoned downtowns and the crowded suburbs. I thought of how divided our nation is, especially by class and race. Yes, we have made tremendous progress since 1964, but how far we are from genuine love. How far we are from a just society—a place where we feed those whom we see as our enemies—a place where we give hospitality to the strangers—a place Martin Luther King, Jr. called "The Beloved Community."

Let love be genuine. Love from the center of who you are. Have the courage to see yourself and the person in front of you, as the redeemed sinners we all are. Have the courage to accept what is and offer the person you are to God so God can use you to mend the broken places in the world.

Community is only possible when we relax. Community is only possible when we put away our masks, and our agendas, and our preconceptions. When we meet someone, it's not, *"How can I keep you in a box—so I can maintain my self-image?"* But, *"How can I see the Christ in you and allow you to see the Christ in me?"*

How can we find genuine love? Remember in *To Kill a Mockingbird* when the white men come in the night and surround the jail where Tom, an African American wrongly accused of a crime, is held? The men are a mob. They do not see Tom. They only see an enemy. They do not know themselves. They are blinded by rage and fear. Scout, a little girl, watches them. Her father tells her to run away and to go home. But Scout doesn't run, and she doesn't fight. Instead she finds a way to love.

She looks at one of the men in the mob and says,

> *Hey, Mister Cunningham. . . . Don't you remember me? . . . I go to school with Walter. He's your boy, ain't he? . . . We brought him home for dinner one time. . . . Tell him "hey" for me, won't you?*[4]

---

4. Harper Lee, *To Kill A Mockingbird* (New York: Warner Books, 1960), 156.

There was a long pause. Then the big man separated himself from the mob, squatted down and took Scout by both her shoulders. *"I'll tell him you said 'hey,' little lady."* Then the mob dispersed.

That's genuine love: Only when we call one another by our true name. Only when we remind one another of how we are connected. Only when we speak and love from the center of who we are will our divisions be healed, and the church will become the place of communion it was created to be.

"*Shalom* Be with You"

> *Jesus came and stood among them and said, "Peace be with you."* . . . *But Thomas (who was called the Twin), one of the twelve, was not with them when Jesus came.* . . . *He said to them, "Unless I see the mark of the nails in his hands, and put my finger in the mark of the nails and my hand in his side, I will not believe."*
> John 20:19, 24–25

The disciples locked the doors to the room because they were afraid. They sat staring at each other because no one knew what to say. No one knew what to do next. How do you follow when your leader is gone? And how do you step out in faith when your leader has just been crucified?

So they sat in the room and held their breath.

Then suddenly Jesus was among them, and he breathed on them. He breathed the same breath God breathed on the waters in creation to bring forth life. Only what he gave them was *shalom.*

Shalom is deep peace. It might be better translated, "wholeness" or "harmony" because *shalom* connects us with all creation. All beings come into right relation with one another. *Shalom* is where the lion and the lamb lie down together. By giving the disciples *shalom,* Jesus doesn't just take away their fears. Jesus brings them into a holy communion. From that place, the disciples can forgive the sins of any, or retain the sins of any because they can see others as Jesus sees others.

The gift of *shalom* is the ultimate consequence of the Incarnation. The Word became flesh and dwells among us—right now. Jesus breathes on the disciples and gives new abundant life, eternal life—right now.

As Gerard Manley Hopkins says, their world is suddenly "charged with the grandeur of God." Even in a small upper room on the outskirts of Jerusalem, Jesus Christ is present. Even when his followers lock the doors because they see their fellow Jews as enemies, Jesus Christ is present.

His presence changes who we are. His presence changes the way we see each other. His presence makes us responsible for one another: If you forgive the sins of any, they are forgiven. If you retain the sins of any, they are retained.

In essence, Jesus is saying to them:

> *From now on I am working through you. From now on, if you want to touch me, touch one another because you are all connected.*

We have all been distraught by the war in Kosovo. It is a testament to how far we are from receiving *shalom*. It's especially tragic that religion is one of the many factors that divides these people. The Orthodox Serbs and the Muslim Albanians hate one another. However we feel about our involvement in Kosovo, let us confess that war is always sinful. Sometimes it may be a necessary sin. Sometimes there are no untainted solutions. We look at the destructiveness of war, and we wonder what to do with the gap between our world and the *shalom* Jesus brings.

Which brings us to Thomas. Thomas knows that he missed out. He was running errands when Jesus gave the other disciples *shalom*. "Unless I see the mark of the nails in his hands . . . I will not believe."

Thomas can't think out the resurrection or the gift of *shalom* in his head. He doesn't know how to get from where he is to where the disciples are. Yes, he can conceive of *shalom*. Yes, he can conceive of the risen Christ; but as T. S. Eliot says, "between the idea and the reality falls the shadow."

How can we span that gap? How can we get from the vision God has for the world to the actual world in which we live? How to get from this gospel reading to the scenes of Kosovo on our television sets?

As I have been thinking of this war, I remembered the novel about World War I, *All Quiet on the Western Front*. In the novel, the narrator, who is German, kills one of his enemies, who is French. As the man is dying, the narrator realizes that his enemy is a husband and a father just like himself. Too late, he realizes that they are brothers; they are connected. They are part of God's *shalom*.

He says to the dead man:

> Comrade, I did not want to kill you. If you jumped in
> here again, I would not do it. . . . But you were only

> an idea to me before, an abstraction that lived in my mind and called forth its appropriate response. It was that abstraction I stabbed. But now, for the first time, I see you are a man like me. . . . Now I see your wife and your face and our fellowship. Forgive me comrade. We always see it too late."

Just as the German soldier cannot believe in an abstract Frenchman who is his brother, Thomas cannot believe in an abstract Jesus. We cannot get to *shalom* with abstractions. When we try, we will either become cynical or hypocritical. Too often we say we love humanity but despise our neighbor. We say we support peace but are filled with aggression toward those around us.

Thomas wants to touch the real deal because he knows that only the concrete touch will save him.

We live in a world where touch is hard, and, therefore, *shalom* seldom occurs. Perhaps the clearest symbol of this is e-mail. It is quick but completely antiseptic. You don't see the person's handwriting; you don't get to finger the stationery. Likewise, we fervently champion great causes like equality without championing any particular person. And, of course, we wage war by pushing buttons that send missiles to targets many miles away. We watch the television coverage and have the illusion of touching these people's lives, but they are only abstractions to us. *Shalom* comes by breaking through abstractions to touch what is real.

"Reach out your hand and put it in my side. Do not doubt but believe." Thomas touched Jesus and received the gift of *shalom.* Legend tells us that he then went to India and passed the touch of *shalom* to those people there. That touch has passed from person to person throughout the ages, for the mystery of Christ is this: When we touch one another in our glory and our woundedness, we touch the risen Christ.

We know from South Africa that *shalom* can be found between people who have hated one another. We know from the miracles in the Truth and Reconciliation Committees there that *shalom* exists. Finally, I remember hearing of one scene where a white man faced the widow of one of the black men he had killed, and the widow said to him, "I just want to know what happened. I just want to know how he died." As the

man told her what he had done, they both cried. He asked her forgive-
ness and they grasped one another's hands and found *shalom*.

I know that this peace is a reality, and I know that we as disciples
of Jesus Christ are called to be the conduits of that peace. We are called
to be touched by Jesus and then become a lifeline of *shalom* that touches the Serbians and the Albanians and the Croats and the Muslims and
the Americans. But our problem is that Thomas was in the same room
as Jesus. And the black woman was in the same room as the South
African man. So how do we touch these people? How do we connect
the Serbian and Albanian hands?

I do not know. I only have guesses. I will list them in ascending
order; the best comes last:

First, if these people are to be less than abstractions, we must find
out who they are. We need to read about Serbia. We need to know about
the conflict going back to the Ottoman Empire. We need to do our best
to put a face on these tragedies so they are not just little dots on the
map we see on CNN.

Second, we can share their suffering. During World War II, Simone
Weil refused to eat more than the soldiers ate. Instead of marches or
protests, let us try fasting for those in Kosovo. Let us try to dilute their
pain by suffering with them. Let us remember that we are all homeless.
We are all refugees. We are all wholly dependent on grace. Let us try
putting our hands into their side by opening ourselves up.

Finally, and most importantly, we are to be people of prayer. Every
day we are to pray for all those who suffer—Serbian, Albanian, and the
NATO forces. We are to pray for Slobadon Milosevic. We are to pray
that these people find a way to touch one another so they do not have
to kill one another. We are to pray for *shalom*—and the way to pray for
shalom is to experience it. The Holy Spirit is contagious: once God's love
is set loose, no military or political force can stop it.

A week later, Jesus comes and stands among them. "Shalom *be with
you.*" he says. Then he said to Thomas, "*Put your finger here and see my
hands. Reach out your hand and put it in my side. Do not doubt but believe.*"

"*Shalom* be with you." Do not doubt but believe.

Curses into Blessings

DEUTERONOMY 30:15–20; PSALM 1; PHILEMON 1–20; LUKE 14:25–33

I have set before you life and death, blessings and curses.
DEUTERONOMY 30:19

We've all had those days—days when everything we touched turned to mud. We feel as if a black cloud is following us. We feel as if we are cursed.

About fifteen years ago, I was driving through Mars Hill, North Carolina, with my two children, then six and two, and a trailer of furniture. The three of us had been on the road for six hours and were going to stay at my parents' house, even though they were not home. We had listened to *Big Bird's Greatest Hits* for almost three hours nonstop, and I had been playing referee for an hour-long wrestling match. Finally we got to my parents' house, and much like Moses, I thought we had reached the promised land. Those six hours certainly felt like forty years.

Halfway up my parents' drive, the car got stuck. The trailer was too heavy. I couldn't go up; I couldn't go down. The two kids started going bananas. I knew I was cursed.

We need to remember those cursed days as we read the Old Testament lesson today because Moses seems to put the burden on our shoulders to choose between being cursed and being blessed. And if we think of his offer literally, it doesn't really make too much sense.

"I have set before you life and death, blessings and curses." It doesn't take too long to choose, does it? While there is a temptation for us to use this passage to congratulate ourselves on choosing life while all those other heathens chose death, I think more is going on. We do have a choice, but it's not quite so simple.

To be cursed is to be so lost that one despairs of ever being found. To be cursed is to feel as if one's heart is frozen and life has lost its energy and purpose. And few of us choose such a state. Rather, we are like Dante who begins his poem, the *Divine Comedy*, with these words, "In the middle of the journey of our life, I came to myself in a dark wood where the straight way was lost." We do not set out to find that dark wood, but one day, there we are.

I have a friend who had a nervous breakdown a few years ago. I was shocked. Betty is a lawyer and seemed to be happily married. She has beautiful children and a nice home. When I went to see her in the hospital and asked her what happened, she said, "Everything seemed so small, I just lost the thread."

Betty had plenty to do, but she had forgotten why anything was worth doing. She felt cut off from any sense of meaning and from the human family. She experienced a deep, deep loneliness—an estrangement from other people, from her emotions, and from God. Life had become a brick wall. She felt cursed.

But there is good news. For underneath our sense of being cursed—beyond those times when we do not know where we are going and feel totally alone—is God's blessing. If we live long enough, each of us will lose the thread, but we need to remember that the blessing is never lost.

Now, our traditional images of blessing may be of a father placing his hands on his eldest son's head as he gives his inheritance, but that is only a partial image of a much more profound primal blessing. To be blessed is to know that you are one of God's beloved. We hear the words of blessing in Isaiah:

> But now thus says the LORD, he who created you . . . he who formed you . . . : Do not fear, for I have redeemed you; I have called you by name, you are mine. . . . Because you are precious in my sight, and honored, and I love you."

To have the blessing is to know that deep in our bones we belong to God and that God is always calling us to grow into greater communion with God and, therefore, with one another. When Moses says, "Choose life." I believe he is calling us to remember our blessing, to recall that the days of curses are not forever, for our destiny is not limited to misfortune. Our destiny is to be the beloved.

I am not saying to deny the pain. When we feel cursed, we should scream and shout just as the psalmist did. But we must not identify ourselves with the pain. Repeatedly Jesus says, "Be not afraid." One way to think of that is, "Do not become your fears," and likewise "Do not become your pain."

This summer I worked as the chaplain in the cancer wing of a hospital. One day I went to see a woman who has stomach cancer. She was in great pain from the therapy. But she turned to me and said, "Don't forget. I am not this disease." She knew that her real self could not be equated with her health or her feelings of being lost. Our cursed days do not have the final word.

"To choose life," then, is to recollect the blessing. As we recollect who we are, we are brought back into relationship with God. Our hearts are unfrozen, and in that still, small voice we pick up the thread of life. We again become God's beloved.

So often we equate being blessed or cursed with what happens to us: do we get stuck going up a mountain, or contract a disease, or get lost in the wilderness, or conversely, become successful?

Moses and the Israelites were on the edge of the promised land, yet we know from scripture, their curses were not done. However many moves we make, however long our exodus takes, there is no absolutely safe place. But that's not the promise. The promise is God's blessing is always, always with us.

I want to tell you a story of a friend of mine who has plenty of reason to feel cursed. Shirley is an alcoholic. She has lost her job and her husband and most of her possessions to the disease of alcoholism. But Shirley had a dream. She dreamed she was in bed and she looked up and saw Jesus standing at the foot of her bed with his arms spread wide open blessing her. She was surprised to see him, but she was especially shocked that he had come to her.

So she asked him, "Why are you here? You know who I am. You know what I've done. Why me? Why me?"

And Christ gazed at her and said, "Because that's who I am."

You and I will have days and weeks and maybe even years when we feel cursed. Like Dante we may find ourselves in a "dark wood where the straight way was lost." But in those moments, choose life. Choose to see the ever-present Christ at your bedside. Choose to hear another passage from Deuteronomy:

> The LORD your God turned the curse into a blessing for you,
> because the LORD your God loved you.

The Eighteenth Camel

 HABAKKUK 3:1–6, 17–19; PSALM 27 OR 27:1–7;
I CORINTHIANS 2:1–11; MATTHEW 5:13–20

You are the salt of the earth. . . . You are the light of the world.
MATTHEW 5:13–14

I remember my first day at seminary. I wasn't really nervous. After more than my share of degrees, I figured I had this school thing down by now. But I was a little perplexed. I had been in the bookstore, but hadn't seen any textbooks. So I asked one of my classmates, named Patsy, where the textbooks were. The next thing I knew, I was sitting and Patsy was standing over me, coming up with an action plan for buying my textbooks: which ones I buy, which ones I could do without, how to get some used ones. And then, I heard all the rumors about the bookstore manager. It took Patsy a half hour to say, "Just go down the steps. The textbooks are downstairs." Later, I asked someone about Patsy, and they said, "Oh, Patsy doesn't make friends. She just takes prisoners."

When the church relates to the outside world, how often do we adopt Patsy's model? Have you noticed the anxious look in the eyes of non-Episcopalians when you speak to them about the church or your faith? Do they involuntarily take a step backward? Maybe it's because they are afraid of being taken prisoner. They are afraid you have an action plan for their lives and you are going to sit them down and stand over them and tell them more than they ever wanted to know.

Our mission as a church is "to restore all people in unity with God and each other in Christ." We will never do that by taking prisoners. Unity does not come from coercion; it comes from transformation. We will never restore anyone to anything by standing over them and telling them the truth of the universe. We are not called to tell people about the faith. We are called to share the faith.

But let's be clear: The opposite reaction is no help. We cannot ignore the world. The church is not a retreat, a refuge. It's not like *Field of Dreams:* We can't say, "If you do nice liturgy, they will be restored."

They won't. As Christians, we cannot take prisoners, nor can we with-draw. We need to find a third way.

In his letter to the Corinthians, Paul gives a hint of what that third way might be.

> *When I came to you brothers and sisters, I did not come pro-claiming the mystery of God to you in lofty words or wisdom. For I decided to know nothing among you except Jesus Christ and him crucified. And I came to you in weakness and in fear and in much trembling.*

There is a lot wrong with the church in Corinth, and Paul could easily take prisoners. He could sit the Corinthians down and lecture them until they agree to become little Pauls. But he does not do so. He does not come as a representative of the triumphant church to stand above people. He comes in weakness. He comes to preach of a Lord who waits for us in our brokenness. But most of all, he comes looking for Jesus Christ in these people.

To see the Christ, we must know who we are looking for. There is no room for any mushy-headed relativism here. We need to be informed by Scripture and tradition so we will know what we see. But we also must go out into the world believing the risen Christ is there waiting to be found in relationship. So long as we are taking prisoners, we will never find him.

In today's gospel, Jesus says we are salt and light. Salt was used as a preservative. It was used as fertilizer, and it was mixed with cow dung was put on top. The salt caused the dung to burn. After a time it had to be replaced. Salt enhances what is innately there, but salt is not salt for itself. Salt cannot salt itself. It is used as an agent of transformation.

Likewise light. Light doesn't turn something into an alien object. It reveals what has been hidden; it illuminates; it dispels the darkness.

As the church, we are called to go into the world with the love of Jesus Christ and reconcile people to God and one another. But we do so not as Christian soldiers marching to war. I saw a billboard in South Carolina that read: "Love Jesus Christ or rot in hell!" That's not the way. That's not salt or light. That's taking prisoners.

And maybe we don't know how to become salt or light, but that's okay: Jesus does not say, "Become salt. Become light." He says, "You are salt—you are light." For we don't do anything but be available for God to work through us.

There is a story about a man who died and left his three sons seventeen camels. He stipulated that the oldest was to get half the camels, the second son a third, and the youngest a ninth. The sons didn't know what to do. They could not fulfill their father's wish with seventeen camels. So they went to a wise man for help. After listening to their story, he thought for a while and then said, "I will loan you a camel—but you must return it when you no longer need it."

The sons went home with eighteen camels. So the eldest takes half—or nine camels. The second son takes his third—or six camels And the youngest takes his ninth—or two camels. 9 + 6 + 2 = 17—So they sent the eighteenth home.

The wise man took no prisoners. Like salt, like light, he provided the key, the catalyst for the sons to move into a new place. Let us find ways to give the eighteenth camel to our world.

In Remembrance of Me
Maundy Thursday

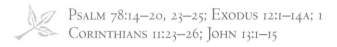 PSALM 78:14–20, 23–25; EXODUS 12:1–14A; 1
CORINTHIANS 11:23–26; JOHN 13:1–15

*So if I , your Lord and Teacher, have washed your feet, you
also ought to wash one another's feet.*
JOHN 13:14

The novelist, Henry James, had one central rule about writing: *"Show
don't tell,"* he would say. Don't tell the reader that this is a sad moment;
show the reader with your descriptions.

Tonight we heard John's version of the Last Supper and Henry
James's words seem especially important, because Jesus is particularly
wordy in John's gospel. He is always saying I AM. *"I am the vine." "I am
the good shepherd." "I am the way."* He repeatedly tries to explain to the
befuddled disciples about his relation to God. *"The Father is in me and I
am in the Father"* and on and on.

But this last night together is not a time for theological explana-
tions. Jesus had no more words left and they wouldn't have understood
them anyway. Jesus said to Peter *"You do not know now what I am doing, but
later you will understand."*

Because Jesus couldn't talk Peter into the mystery of how interconnected we are through God's love, he had to touch him to show him.
Instead of talking about the body of Christ, Jesus touched their bodies
with his. Our translation says, *"Unless I wash you, you have no share with
me."* But the word *"share"* really means *"to be partnered with"* or even *"to
have a heritage with."*

The way to be partnered with Christ, the way to be connected to
him in the unknown future is to be touched by him and in turn touch
the world in his name.

In Jesus' day, when you came to someone's house one of their servants would wash your feet. Certainly this was an issue of cleanliness.
In a world of sandals, people's feet were more than just dusty. But it was

also an entrance rite. Your feet were washed, and then you could come into the inner rooms. Your feet were washed, and then you were no longer a stranger but connected to the household. Jesus washes the disciples' feet so that they will be part of his heart. Regardless of what happens he washes their feet to take them into God's inner household.

You know, so much of memory is tactile. I remember so many of my departed loved ones by the smell of their clothes or the feel of their hands. My grandmother has been dead for thirty years but I can still remember how her cheek felt when I kissed her. And I can still remember the smell of her house when she made breakfast. She cooked buckwheat pancakes and made coffee so black the spoon stood up in the cup. I smell those smells anywhere anytime, and I remember her.

Jesus loved the disciples to the end by touching them so they would remember HIM. Every time they entered someone's house, and their feet were washed, they would remember Him—they would be re-membered to him.

Just as he said, whenever you sit at a table and break bread in my name, do this for the remembrance of me. Do this and you will remember how I touched you. It's no wonder that as soon as she saw the risen Christ, Mary Magdalene grabs his feet. It's no wonder that Thomas said without the touch, I will not believe. It's the touch they remembered.

In time, the disciples discovered that touch is everywhere. To their surprise and delight, they found that when they washed one another's feet, they washed the feet of Jesus. Just as when they broke bread and drank wine in his name, it didn't matter where they were. It didn't matter what year it was. He was there. Do this for the remembrance of me.

If we are to know Jesus in our lives, it probably won't come through thinking about him. It will come through doing these things for the remembrance of him. It will come through gathering around tables like this one. And telling the story over and over. And eating the bread and drinking the wine—so that we discover this church is that Upper Room. Two thousand five is the year Jesus came into Jerusalem.

If we are to know Jesus in our world tomorrow or next week or next month, it probably won't come through thinking about him. After we have eaten the bread and drunk the wine, we are sent into the world to touch our brothers and sisters in the name of Jesus. For the remembrance of him. We are called to bend down as servants to the little ones of the earth, just as he bent down to his disciples.

If we are to remember him, it won't be by being served, but by serving. Do this—means do for others as I have done for you.

Michael Mayne, who is the dean of Westminster Cathedral, writes of going to Calcutta to visit one of Mother Teresa's homes for the dying. The sister in charge was Sister Luke. She showed him the ward where the poor were brought in from the streets.

Michael Mayne says Sister Luke took him to a small cubicle. An old woman, who had just been brought in, was lying in a wooden trough half filled with water. Two Missionaries of Charity were gently washing her clean and comforting her. Above the trough, nailed to the wall just above her body was a simple sign that said "The Body of Christ."

We gather tonight not just to remember Jesus on that night long ago. We gather tonight to remember that Jesus is in every man and woman. When you wash your neighbor's feet tonight, you wash the feet of Jesus. And when you encounter your neighbor in the streets of Athens or Watkinsville or any city, your neighbor's feet are the feet of Jesus. You have been invited into the inner rooms of Jesus' heart so that you may invite all God's children.

At the very end of the evening, Jesus asked them, *"Do you know what I have done to you?"* Of course, they didn't know then. And of course, most of the time we don't know now. But what he has done is to connect us to him forever. What he has done is placed himself inside every person. What he has done is given us the gift to remember him if we will only do this for the remembrance of him.

Paradise in Community

 PSALM 68:1–20; ACTS 16:16–34; REVELATION
22:12–14, 16–17, 20; JOHN 17:20–26

And let everyone who is thirsty come.
REVELATION 22:17

This is an age test. How many of you remember the Joni Mitchell song—"Woodstock"? That's right—the one made famous by Crosby, Stills, and Nash. As I remember it—here's the refrain:

We are stardust; we are golden
And we've got to get ourselves back to the garden.

One of the many reasons the song was popular is that it names our hunger for a return to the garden. A hunger for a return to innocence—to a time and place that is more simple and quieter. We imagine that being spiritual means escaping all the complexity and confusion of today. The goal is to return to the innocence of Eden where we walk with God in the morning and there is not that sense of separation between us and creation.

We are home. We know the names of all living things. We are with the people we love. And all the people that drive us crazy are somewhere else—perhaps with a lower longitude. It's peaceful and serene.

Now, I doubt that Joni Mitchell cared too much whether she was biblically correct. She probably didn't dig out her copy of Revelation to see if indeed the final vision of what is to come includes a return to Eden. However, if we haven't read our Revelation in a long time it may come as a shock to us that the Bible offers a very different picture of the end of history: we never get back to the garden.

Because God is involved in history, we are not going back to where we started but to a new place, a surprising place. The culmination of history is a large—bustling—crowded—active CITY. That's right. In spite of the fact that we want the final destination to be

40

Walden Pond, we are headed for New York City or, more precisely, the New Jerusalem.

Jean-Paul Sartre said *"Hell is other people."* But he got it wrong. *"Heaven is other people." Paradise is in community.* God's vision for God's people is that they learn to live together in harmony.

In the Gospel today, we hear Jesus' prayer that his followers "may be one." As the psalm says, *"How very good and pleasant it is when kindred live together in unity!"* The goal of creation is not a private relation with God. The Christian vision is not merely me and Jesus. The final vision is where all God's people are one. The final vision is a holy communion, a city alive with a diverse community.

The wonderful part about the heavenly city is that we don't blur our differences. It's not as if we are going to put on uniforms and all look the same. Unity is not uniformity. No—unity comes from discovering the love that connects us all. We find that what binds us is more than what separates us.

Or to put it another way, unity comes when we come to delight in our differences, because those differences mirror the greatness of the Creator. When we are connected to God, we are connected to each other. And the truth is, if we do not find that water table—our communion seldom lasts.

We try to build community out of common interests, but when those interests change we find ourselves alone again. Now let's get real here. Take a moment and think of the people who drive you up the wall. Think of the people that represent all that you cannot stand in the world. Think of the people who are everything you are not. The streets of the heavenly city are filled with them.

They are all there. Depending on your politics, we're talking about Bill Clinton or George Bush. We're talking about Marilyn Manson or Wayne Newton. We're talking about Steve Spurrier—Madonna—Jerry Springer. We're talking about Al Frankin and Bill O'Reilly; Bishop Spong and Jerry Falwell. We're talking about everyone who wants to be there in this city rubbing shoulders, praising God, being in community.

We hear the vision and look at our condition and shake our heads over the difference. Our world has become like amoeba—we divide and divide and divide and then we subdivide. Every time we encounter a deep difference, the tendency is to demonize the other and then move away. The tendency is to label others as evil or depraved or sick or sinful or whatever label works. And then to remove them from our presence. Is it any wonder that some of our inner cities have become ghost towns?

And let's don't leave the church off the hook. In the history of the Episcopal Church—that is since the American Revolution—forty groups have split off to form their own denomination. We have such a hard time with community, is it any wonder we think of heaven as Walden Pond instead of the New Jerusalem?

So what are we to do? The fundamental move for us to make is to realize that this is God's deep desire for us and then for us in turn to embrace that desire for ourselves.

First, God's desire for us. Let's go back to the text. The author of Revelation writes:

> It is I, Jesus, who sent my angel to you with this testimony to the churches.
> I am the root and the descendant of David, the bright morning star.
> The Spirit and the bride say, "Come." . . . And let everyone who is thirsty come.

Jesus holds up the vision of the New Jerusalem and then like a mother to her children urges—extols—pleads with creation to live into it. The word Jesus speaks over and over again is "come": *Let everyone who is thirsty come.* Just as the bridegroom yearns for the bride—so the Christ yearns for humanity to come—to stop being places like our contemporary cities and become the New Jerusalem. "Come," the ascended Jesus cries—"Come home to me."

The truth is, sometimes we forget that love is what matters. We forget that God loves us and that our only home in all of creation is with the source of that love. When that happens, we turn to our lives of isolation and loneliness and death. When we forget that all of life is rooted in responding to God's love for God's creation, then we make the world a jumble of things and our lives secure prisons that insulate us from the source of life. We feel secure, but we don't feel at home.

But whenever I have been in that place, love is the only thing that melts my heart. A word—a touch—a gesture—a child being free in the world of grace. And I long for that city—I long to belong—I long for communion.

Therefore, our job is to echo Jesus' plea. We are to echo God's desire for us. Just as he calls for us to come, so we are to pray for him to come to us. Because we do not know how to get to him. We do not know how to build the heavenly city—only God knows. The New Jerusalem is a gift from God freely given if God's children long for it. Jesus issues the invitation for us to come and waits for us to invite him into our world.

The truth is the New Jerusalem is at the end of time and right now. Thomas Merton says, "In one sense we are always traveling. . . . In another sense we have already arrived."[5]

That means even as we long for the heavenly city and to be one we have glimpses along the way.

In 1913 the surviving Civil War veterans gathered for the fiftieth anniversary of the battle of Gettysburg. At one point they had a reenactment of Pickett's Charge.

The Union soldiers took their places among the rocks on Seminary Ridge and the Confederate soldiers stood on the farmland below. The Southern veterans moved forward but instead of "rifles and bayonets" they held "canes and crutches."

When the Confederate troops neared the Union lines, they let out one long rebel yell. And then the world was filled with grace because the two armies embraced one another—some in gray, some in blue—all children of God—all citizens of the New Jerusalem.

On that day the kingdom of God drew near. You and I will never get back to the garden but this is the good news—the heavenly city is all about us. And Jesus says to us what he has been saying for two thousand years:

Come—please come.

---

5. Thomas Merton, *A Thomas Merton Reader* (Garden City, NY: Doubleday, 1974), 513.

Turning Round Right

Sermons of Conversion

Trick or Treat

ISAIAH 42:1–7; JAMES 2:5–9, 12–17;
MATTHEW 10:32–42

> *[My servant] will not grow faint or be crushed until he has
> established justice in the earth.*
> ISAIAH 42:4

Tomorrow night is the big night—the only night of the year when all
those warnings about candy and your teeth go out the window. When
I was a kid, I remember how excited I got over Halloween. My sister
and I would spend days mapping out the best route to take. We kept a
mental scorecard of who gave us M&Ms and who gave us apples. And
we would start out as soon as dinner was over. As the evening wore on,
and our bags got heavier, we'd go to houses we knew and broadly hint
that we'd like to rest. Hints like, "Can I come in and sit down?"

What I remember most is that the streets were full of children and
the lights from all the houses were blazing. If you stood back and just
watched the rows of houses, the doors opened and closed like giant fire-
flies in the autumn night.

Now I look at Halloween differently. Often I am in my house
greeting those strange faces that come to my door. Now I worry that
some of the candy in their bags may no longer be safe. Now I worry
about these kids as they turn and go into the darkness. Now I pray that
nothing bad happens to them.

I don't want to overly romanticize the past and I don't want to
lament over our present day. But I want to say that Halloween might be
like the mission Isaiah has in mind for us. We are to "faith-fully bring
forth justice." We are to be

> *A light to the nations,*
> *to open the eyes that are blind,*
> *to bring out the prisoners from the dungeon,*
> *from the prison those who sit in the darkness.*

We all know that like Isaiah we too live in darkness: one in every four of our people lives in poverty. Many are denied basic medical care. We can transplant a baboon's liver into a person, but we can't adequately feed our people, and we cannot give everyone a place to sleep.

If we focus on the ways our society promotes injustice in its very structures, we may become paralyzed. Let's not think of institutions; let's think of people.

Dorothy Day, one of the great champions for social justice, gives us a clue. She once said that her fear was that when she got to heaven, God would meet her at the entrance and ask, "Where are the others?" Dorothy Day knew there is no private salvation. The kingdom of God is not about your or my holiness; it's about bringing the whole body of Christ into the light.

So our question is also: where are the others? In Isaiah's words, where are those whose reeds have been bruised so they can no longer sing? Where are those whose light is only dimly burning? Where are those locked in the prison of poverty?

Once I asked a Portuguese friend of mine what she thought of America and she said, "It's a wonderful country, but you are such lonely people. Everyone lives in their little boxes."

We wall in the light in our boxes and fear the dark outside. "Where are the others?" They are in the darkness. But the Lord has called all of us to be a light. We cannot grow faint or be crushed until justice is established. What, then, can we do?

Back to Halloween.

Injustice is systemic. It is hard to see. But we can see its products and we can attack them. We can begin with the darkness of poverty. Those of us who have food and shelter—our basic needs met—don't want to look at those in the darkness. But they are out there. And sooner or later they will come to our doors and knock.

When they come and we first see their faces, we will be frightened. They might look like pirates or witches or monsters. They will ask, "Trick or Treat": "Trick" = Do you want to repeat the cycle of violence? "Treat" = Together can we look for grace?

"Trick or Treat?" "Violence or Grace?" "Poverty or Justice?" "Death or Life?"

Where are the others? They are at our doors. We can only dispel the darkness by opening those doors; we can only share the light by inviting the others in.

What if every night were Halloween? What if the only way to light our streets was by opening our doors so that the light would stream out of each doorway and flood the streets? And those others would come and ask for what they need. At first they would look scary, but if we found a way to move from "Trick" to "Treat" we could ask them to hold out their bags and fill them with gifts. Then they would take their masks off. And we would see them as they are.

"I am the Lord, I have called you . . . to open the eyes that are blind." The blind eyes are our eyes. Our task is to share our wealth and to oppose a few having so much while so many have so little. Our gift is our money and our privileges. But the gift of the others is to open our eyes—to cleanse our sight. For brothers and sisters, behind those masks that make us so frightened, behind what looks like pirates and ghosts and monsters—lies the face of Christ.

When they come to our doors, we will not at first recognize them. They may look like strangers. But their voices will be Christ's voice asking, "Trick or Treat?" "Violence or Grace?" "Poverty or Justice?" "Death or Life?"

Don't Skate Alone

 Exodus 20:1–17; Psalm 19:7–14; Romans 7:13–25; John 2:13–22

> *For I do not do the good I want, but the evil I do not want is what I do. . . . Wretched man that I am! Who will rescue me from this body of death?*
> Romans 7:19, 24

If Lent is a time for confession, I confess I am fascinated by Tonya Harding. I've read the magazines, watched the news, and when I go to Kroger, I can't wait to see what the National Enquirer has to say about her. I am fascinated for many reasons, but the most notable is that Tonya Harding is a barometer for our culture. She is an icon for the dark side of the American dream.

Tonya Harding reminds us of the dangers of our worship of individualism: Think about our picture of heroism; it's one person on, we believe, some solitary quest. The Lone Ranger, Batman, Superman, Ahab of *Moby Dick*, Cool Hand Luke, Randle McMurphy of *One Flew over the Cuckoo's Nest,* and the best example, Will Kane of the film *High Noon.* The hero is a stranger. Often he is an orphan without a past, and he doesn't need anyone. It's just him and the world, and he fights by his own rules.

We can believe whatever we want about the Olympics and how sweet Nancy Kerrigan is, but Tonya Harding is the dark side that we don't like to see. The dark side that says, "I don't need anyone and I'm going to win at all costs."

And so last Friday I turned on the TV with great anticipation. Tonya was announced, and then minute after minute passed and she didn't show. Then finally she came. But she only skated thirty seconds and the whole thing fell apart. It fell apart because there is a shadow that follows Tonya Harding. A dark side that keeps ambushing her and destroying her best efforts. She skates faster and faster and smiles harder and harder. But she can't skate fast enough or smile hard enough. Her shadow creeps up, and there she is again— in the middle of the ice with the whole world watching as she falls apart. You could see it in her face, saying, *"Here I am again—it never works out the way I planned."*

Now, what does this have to do with Scripture or church or Jesus Christ?

Everything. Tonya Harding is an icon for what ails us in this country because her dark side is that she believes that she is *alone.* It's just her and the ice—a solitary quest. The only rules that count are the ones the judges use to award points. We can skate faster and faster and smile harder and harder, but if we believe we are alone, if we take on the world, solo, then we will always end up like Tonya: crying in the middle of the ice.

Listen to the question St. Paul asks in today's epistle. It's also Tonya's question, and it's our question:

> *For I do not do what I want, but I do the very thing I hate. . . .*
> *Wretched man that I am! Who will rescue me from this body of*
> *death?*

If I depend only on myself, I will get lost and will end up doing the very thing I hate. We like to think of the hero on this solitary quest for the prize, the gold medal. But we need to remember that as humans our capacity for self-deception is endless. And if we depend solely on ourselves to find the way, we may end up lashing out at anyone who threatens our success. We may end up hitting Nancy Kerrigan on the knee.

"Who will rescue me?" God will. Our God is the God who brought the Israelites out of Egypt, the God who has made a covenant with us, and who has given us the Law, the Torah, to live by.

Torah literally means "the finger pointing the way." This morning we read about the Ten Commandments, and these are part of the Torah. These are one of the ways we stay connected to God. The commandments are a foundation on which our common lives can be built.

In his book, *Habits of the Heart,* Robert Bellah describes a woman named Sheila: Sheila has her own religion—she calls it "Sheilaism." Sheila doesn't go to church. She doesn't write any commandments in her heart. She just listens to "My own little voice."

How much of our society does that describe? *Do your own thing. I have my truth—you have yours. If it feels good, do it.* And the bottom line becomes whatever gets us closer to winning the gold. If we have no foundation, then we will end up doing the very thing we hate. Like Tonya Harding we will self-destruct.

Who will rescue us? God will. God has given these commandments as a lifeboat. They will not solve all our problems, but they will keep us from creating our private hells as we quest for some gold medal. The commandments give us a map—some rules to go by so that we do not always get lost. The commandments root our lives in what God's intention is for all God's people. No one can rescue himself or herself from the human capacity to sin, but the commandments give us a base—a foundation—a lifeline connecting us to the almighty so that we are not alone.

And so this Lent, let's stop trying to be the Lone Ranger. Instead, let's begin to build a new Easter life on God's foundations. Let's move beyond "Sheilaism" or Tonya Harding and take God's law to heart. For if we place our feet on the commandments, and place our hands in the hands of Jesus Christ, when we fall on the ice, we will not feel like Tonya Harding. For our faith will not be in our own ability to win the gold, but in God's faithfulness to show us the way through the law and to be with us through the love of Jesus Christ.

Curing Mammon Illness

 Amos 8:4–7 (8–12); Psalm 138; I Timothy
2:1–8; Luke 16:1–13

> *Whoever is faithful in a very little is faithful also in much;*
> *and whoever is dishonest in a very little is dishonest also in*
> *much. . . . You cannot serve God and wealth.*
> Luke 16:10, 13

Martin Buber tells this story of a Jewish mystic's disciple:

> The disciple wants to fast, so he decides not to eat or
> drink any thing for a week. He makes it through six
> days, and on the last day—tormented with thirst—he
> almost gives in and goes to the spring to take a drink.
> But he overcomes the temptation and turns around.
> As he is walking away, he says to himself: "Maybe I
> am too proud. Perhaps it would be better for my soul
> if I took a drink." So he goes back to the spring, but
> once there he is no longer thirsty, so he says, "Why
> take a drink!" and returns home.
>
> The next day he goes to see his master and tells
> him of his success. The master looks at him and says,
> "Patchwork!" Patchwork means the result may be
> right, but it doesn't come from a unified sense of who
> this person is. The disciple is not acting from his center
> but is only responding to a variety of voices.[6]

Our lives and world are so complex. It often feels as if our main
activities are all patchwork. As we say, "I feel scattered." "I feel at loose
ends." We say, "I am meeting myself coming and going." Patchwork.
Jesus says:

---

6. Thomas Merton, *Thomas Merton in Alaska* (New York: New Directions, 1981), 149.

> *Whoever is faithful in a very little is faithful also in much; and whoever is dishonest in a very little is dishonest also in much. . . . No slave can serve two masters. . . . You cannot serve God and wealth* [or as we used to translate it, "God and mammon"].

If we are to believe in Christ, which means to be grasped by him, we must stop being so scattered. We must stop trying to paste together our divided lives and instead live from the center of who we are.

You cannot serve God and mammon. John Howie says our culture suffers from "mammon illness." Mammon illness has three symptoms:

First, we are always frantic. We are always anxious. We are permanently distracted. Our culture is addicted to stimulation. We have filled our space with gadgets upon gadgets. And yes, there is great benefit to all this stuff. We can do tasks faster and we can be connected to one another in amazing ways, but the downside is that we are seldom focused on one thing. We talk on the phone while we are watching a soccer game; we work on our laptops while we are riding in an automobile. I spent the night with a friend recently. When I came down to breakfast, he was watching the weather channel and listening to *Morning Edition* and reading the paper and talking to his wife.

There is a story about a group of disciples who were on their way to see a wise monk. One of the younger members asked one of the older ones what he planned to ask the monk, and the older one said, "Nothing. I just want to see him tie his shoes." *"Whoever is faithful in a very little is faithful also in much."* The attraction of the monk is that he knew who he was, so every act is an expression of that core self.

The second symptom of mammon illness is we suffer a split life. We compartmentalize our varied roles and activities. So we think being a Christian is about going to church and helping the church run. But we think Christianity has little to do with being a business person, or a spouse, or a parent.

We need to remember that our Southern ancestors who owned slaves were also Christians. And all the champions of *apartheid* in South Africa were Christians. Most of the Nazis were Christians. You cannot serve two masters. We are called to love the Lord our God with all our heart and all our soul and all our mind, and to love our neighbor as our self. All else will follow.

Life becomes complicated when our lives are patchwork. There are so many competing demands on us that we must put God first.

People would come to Jesus and ask him all sorts of requests: Will you give me sight? Make me walk. Make me hear. And what he asks them is: "Do you believe?" In other words, "Do you love with all your heart and soul and mind?"

All else follows. If we don't remember this, we'll be like the shrewd servant who is not only corrupt but gets praised by his corrupt master, so that finally no one remembers what it is to be faithful. We must have our bearings internally, for if we don't, we will succumb to the glitter of the world.

Finally, because of mammon illness, we don't feel. We are numb. We are not passionate about our lives. We are so driven by being efficient that we don't focus on the little task in front of us.

So we eat "fast food" instead of enjoying a meal. We fill our lives with television instead of any real art or drama. We long for some real encounter or some sense of being alive. Yet so much of the time it seems our lives are shadows. Maybe that's why people go bungee jumping. Maybe that's why we crave so much stimulation because we want to feel something. Jesus calls us to enter into his passion. Instead of trying to feel from the outside in, we need to feel from the inside out.

Our Lord is calling us to be cured of mammon illness. And it doesn't require a herculean effort. You don't have to go to Walden Pond to do it.

This passage by Thomas Merton helps:

> God places in my heart a "yes" to Him. And that is God's secret. He knows my "yes" even when I am not saying it. My destiny in life . . . is to uncover this "yes" so that my life is totally and completely a "yes" to God, a complete assent to God.[7]

We do not need to go to India to do great works of service to be a good Christian. We need to remember who we are. We need to uncover our "yes" to God. We need to remember that we are Christ's own. We

---

7. Thomas Merton, *Thomas Merton in Alaska: The Alaskan Conferences, Journals and Letters* (New York: New Directions Publishing Corporation, 1989), 154.

need to feel that love that God has for us and to recapture that blessing that God is always giving us. Then do each small task from that place, for the spiritual life is a life of habits, a life of disciplines, small things, everyday acts.

We should ask ourselves if the small acts we do come from our "yes" to God, or if they are patchwork. Small acts—like treating people at the grocery store with respect, looking into the eyes of the check-out teller, remembering that the person who takes your change is a child of God—a Christ-bearer.

Small acts—like caring for our possessions or to stop seeing possessions as disposable. Thinking about what we really need to be who we are. Then giving up the rest. Just because the advertisements say we need a new car doesn't mean we need one. To focus on what is in front of us. If we are mowing the lawn, then mow the lawn. If we are eating, then eat.

Whoever is faithful in a very little is faithful also in much.

Let us remember, the Word is made flesh and dwells among us. Every moment of every day, God is saying "yes" to us. Every moment of every day, God longs for us to say "yes" back.

Made to Hold the Light

Deuteronomy 18:15–20; Psalm 111;
I Corinthians 8:1b–13; Mark 1:21–28

> *Just then there was in their synagogue a man with an unclean
> spirit, and he cried out, "What have you to do with us, Jesus
> of Nazareth? Have you come to destroy us?"... But Jesus
> rebuked him, saying, "Be silent, and come out of him!"*
> Mark 1:23–25

Ursula LeGuin writes fantasy books. In her best-known work, *The
Earthsea Trilogy*, she tells the story of a young wizard named Ged. In the
second volume, Ged goes on a quest to find a magical ring. The ring is
held by the priestess of a dark region. She is called "Arha," which means
the "one who has been devoured."

Arha was taken from her mother at birth and brought up to attend
to the powers of darkness—called the Nameless Ones—that reside
underground in tombs beneath the city. She alone can go into the dark
tombs. She alone experiences the terrifying negative presence. She wanders in a maze where there is never light.

In looking for the ring, Ged becomes lost in this underground
maze. He almost dies of thirst, yet Arha saves his life by sneaking him
food and water. One day Ged says to her: "You are like a lantern
swathed and covered, hidden away in a dark place. Yet the light shines:
they could not put out the light. They could not hide you. As I know
the light, as I know you, I know your name—you are TENAR."

And thus, Tenar is free. She is no longer possessed by the Nameless
Ones. She no longer identifies herself as "One who has been devoured."
She knows who she is and she is able to leave the darkness and reenter
the world as her true self.

I thought of LeGuin's novel this week as I have been wrestling with
the gospel for today. It is so difficult to talk about demon possession
today. Either we sensationalize it—and we find ourselves in the land of
the occult or in the movie, *The Exorcist*. Or we trivialize it so that any
psychological disturbance becomes demonic.

We either turn Jesus into a magician or a therapist—and he is neither. Jesus is the Christ. And the Christ has come so that we might remember who we are and who God is.

So what are we to do with today's gospel? Jesus encounters a man who is possessed. And the demonic spirit asks, "What have you to do with us, Jesus of Nazareth? Have you come to destroy us?"

Jesus commands the demon to come out. If we make this story too sensational, we'll miss the point. Yes, people can become possessed. And yes, exorcism is a rite that exists in the Episcopal Church, but these are extreme cases. If we focus on the extreme forms of demonic possession, we will miss how the gospel relates to our lives. The point here is the demons' questions: *"What have you to do with us, Jesus of Nazareth? Have you come to destroy us?"*

And the answer is *"Yes."* Jesus has come into the world to confront the dark powers. And we don't have to roll our eyes or shake convulsively or have projectile vomiting in order to know that dark powers can and do creep into our lives—powers that make us forget who we are and that drive us underground.

So often we find ourselves like Tenar. We have forgotten our true name. And we find ourselves living far from home, not remembering where we belong, living with the Nameless Ones and feeling unconnected to God and to one another. These dark forces take many shapes: we may know them as depression or addiction or greed or fear or selfishness or rage. But when they possess us, two things can happen:

> One. We feel alone. We feel as if we have lost our way home.
> Two. We make others feel that way.

Either we go into the darkness or we push others into the darkness.

I think that each of us knows that the world is in trouble, but most of the time we don't know what to do about it. We confront those demons in ourselves or in others, and we feel as if we have to do something. So we read a book or take a course or go into therapy or do good works or go shopping, or whatever it is that stops the voices saying that something is wrong.

But what we are looking for is the one with authority over the demons. Authority does not come from possessions or wealth or knowledge or certificates. Jesus has none of those. Jesus has authority because he is the light of the world.

The demon cries: *"What have you to do with us, Jesus of Nazareth? Have you come to destroy us?"*

And Jesus' actions shout, *"Yes, yes I have."* For the Christ has come to remind us of who we are: children of the light marked as Christ's own forever:

"What have you to do with us, Jesus of Nazareth? Have you come to destroy us?"

Yes, yes, he has, because Jesus knows our names—because the Christ sees our true self. And he calls us to join him in his light. That's the authority he has: the authority to remind us of who we are and who God is.

"Be silent," Jesus says to the demons, and, *"and come out of him."* For I am claiming this one as my own and bringing this child home.

Yes, evil does exist in our world, but if we believe in the resurrected Christ, then we are called to use this authority with one another and with the world. We are called to reach to those in darkness who feel they have been devoured or who feel they are nameless. We are to remind them and ourselves who we all are: Christ's own children—marked and sealed forever.

LeGuin ends her novel with this. Ged says:

> *"Listen, Tenar. The evil is poured out. It is done. It is buried in its own tomb. You were never made for cruelty and darkness; you were made to hold the light, as a lamp burning holds and gives light."* . . . *He leapt up onto the pier and turned, holding his hand to her. "Come," he said smiling, and she rose and came. She walked beside him up the white streets . . . holding his hand, like a child coming home.*[8]

---

8. Ursula K. LeGuin, *The Tombs of Atuan* (New York: Aladdin, 2001), 180.

Can't Buy You Love

 AMOS 5:6–7, 10–15; PSALM 90 OR 90:1–8, 12;
HEBREWS 3:1–6; MARK 10:17–27 (28–31)

> *Jesus, looking at him, loved him and said, "You lack one thing: go, sell what you own, and give the money to the poor, and you will have treasure in heaven; then come, follow me."*
> MARK 10:21

We get to the end of the story of the rich man and hope it's not the end. It doesn't turn out right. This is the only time in Mark's gospel that Jesus calls someone, but he doesn't respond.

We know how it's supposed to go: Jesus says, *"Leave your jobs; leave your families; come, follow me."* And—whoosh—they're on the road. The old life is behind and their new life has begun. But this doesn't follow the script. This time the man *"was shocked and went away grieving."* What happened to our happy ending?

Well, to tell the truth, this encounter doesn't get off to a very good start. The man asks a question, but it's an upside-down question: *"What must I do to inherit eternal life?"*

It's an upside-down question because we don't *do* anything about inheritances. Perhaps the answer is, *"Don't disappear,"* or, *"Show up after the death."* What is there finally *to do?*

Eternal life, like an inheritance, isn't earned. It's grace, given to us because we are connected to someone who has it to give. We don't need to flatter Jesus by calling him *"Good Teacher."* We don't need to show our Ten Commandments merit badges. Yes, Jesus does rattle off some of the commandments, but you have the feeling he is humoring this person. Certainly Jesus knew that you don't obey the commandments to earn eternal life. You obey because you are in covenant with, in love with, God. I don't give my mother birthday or Christmas presents to earn her love. I give her presents because I love her.

"What must I do to inherit eternal life?" Don't do anything. Just stay in touch with the one who has it to give.

But this mystery is beyond the rich man. He doesn't get it. He lives in a first-century corporate world: a world of accomplishments and actions. He is accustomed to being an important person: a mover and a shaker. And Jesus knows this. He must know this because he humors the man.

"What must I do to inherit eternal life?" Jesus could have said, *"Simple. Stay in touch with me."* But he doesn't. The *Jerusalem Bible* says, "Jesus looked steadily at him and loved him."

Maybe Jesus knows that the man is tired of Perrier water and instead thirsts for the water of life.

Maybe Jesus knows that the man has reached the limits of what he can earn and wants to enter the land of grace but doesn't know what that means.

Jesus looked steadily at him and was filled with love for him. Jesus sees all the way through—all the way to what holds the man back. Jesus knows that love means being honest and taking someone seriously. Jesus tells the man the truth, but it's not the truth the man wanted to hear.

"You lack one thing; go, sell what you own, and give the money to the poor, and you will have treasure in heaven; then come, follow me."

No wonder the man was shocked and went away grieving. One commentator rightly points out that the opposite of rich is not poor. The opposite of rich is free. That's why the Beatitudes say, *"Happy are you who are poor, for yours is the kingdom of God"* (Luke 6:20).

If we believe that every good thing has to be earned, we are never free to accept grace. So Jesus says to the disciples: *"How hard it is for those who have riches to enter the kingdom of God!"*

Hard because money gives us the illusion of self-sufficiency and control. We believe that money is power—the power to control our lives and our environment. Our culture tells us that *You are what you own.* And so, like the rich man, we, too, end up asking such upside-down questions. Questions like, "How much money do I need to feel important? How rich must I be to compensate for the love I cannot feel? What must I do to inherit eternal life?"

So this passage is about money and about making an idol of money. However, because we can make an idol of anything, this passage is about more than money. It's about how hard it is to let go of our idols and experience the freedom of grace. The rich man doesn't argue with Jesus. He knows he has heard the truth, but he cannot let go.

Transformation occurs when something old falls apart, and we step into a confusing in-between place, and then live into the new life of freedom.

It's hard to make that step. For this man it's his wealth; he cannot imagine a world where you don't need to pay for grace. He cannot imagine being loved for just being a child of God.

And so he cannot, and will not let go. But anything can hold us from experiencing eternal life. Anything can keep us from accepting our inheritance as children of God. Prejudice, anger, jealousy, addiction, pride—anything.

Now at this point, maybe you feel like the disciples when they cry out, *"Who can be saved?"*

If it's so hard to let go of wealth or whatever else it is that binds us, then what in the world are we to do? I don't want to make this too simple. C. S. Lewis once said, "All things are possible. It is even possible to get a large camel through the small eye of a needle, but it will be extremely hard on the camel."

But let's go back to the question: *"What must I do to inherit eternal life?"*

I repeat. The answer is hard, but simple: *"Don't disappear."*

You see, the inheritance is given at unexpected times. And it's not given to rich men or rich women, because they can't receive it. No, it's given to people like Mary Magdalene. After the crucifixion, all the rich folks are far away in their safe houses. No one is clamoring after Jesus now. No one is coming to him to flatter him with *Good Teacher* now.

Mary goes to the tomb without her good deeds. She doesn't have a Ten Commandments merit badge. She goes because her Lord's love commands her to go. What must she do to inherit eternal life? Don't disappear. Show up. Be where he is.

Eternal life doesn't come from us, or our money, or our deeds. It comes from *him*.

Look—Weep—Live

 Ezekiel 37:1–3 (4–10), 11–14; Psalm 130;
Romans 6:16–23; John 11:(1–17) 18–44

> *He cried with a loud voice, "Lazarus, come out!" The dead*
> *man came out, his hands and feet bound with strips of cloth,*
> *and his face wrapped in a cloth. Jesus said to them, "Unbind*
> *him, and let him go."*
> John 11:43–44

It's hard to admit we are at a dead end. We come to a place that feels like a stone tomb, and our mind starts saying, *maybe, maybe, maybe.* Or we are like Martha: "Lord, if you had been here, my brother would not have died." We want to rewrite the past. We want to spend our time creating alternate realities. If only I had done this; if only he hadn't done that.

Dead ends are hard to face. I mean death itself and the living death. I mean Lazarus who has been in the tomb for four days, and I mean the parts of our selves and of our lives that die, the parts we wall off so that we live a partial life.

Today's gospel is about resurrection. It's a prelude to Good Friday, Holy Saturday, and Easter. It shows us that the first step toward resurrection is to see where we are.

Alan Jones says that there are three stages in the spiritual life: *Look. Weep. Live.*[9]

To look: to let go of our excuses and our clichés. To stop saying, it's all for the best and *just* admit death stinks.

Like all of us, the only solution Martha and Mary can think of is to avoid death. When I was in the eighth grade our science teacher showed us a film about folks who would freeze people who had dire diseases, thinking that one day we would find a cure and then thaw them out and they could keep living. Too often that's the way we deal with our lives. We freeze off parts of our selves. We freeze off relationships that don't work and live a half life.

---

9. Alan Jones, *Soul Making: The Desert Way of Spirituality* (New York: Harper and Row, 1985), 22.

There is no way around the tomb. The way to resurrection is by going through the tomb. There is no Easter without Good Friday. As Henry David Thoreau says, "it is life at the bone where it is sweetest." So the first step to resurrection is to *look*—to embrace where we are, regardless of how it smells.

What are we to do after that? We weep. We let the tears run down our faces. We let our sorrow sink all the way into our hearts. Jesus heard about the death of his friend and he shuddered and wept. He wept because he missed his friend. And his tears joined with those of Mary and Martha.

Someone once said, "In sorrow there are no strangers." There is just the communion of tears. For the truth is that if we love, we will weep. Love always opens us up to suffer—always. That's why in Dante's *Inferno,* Satan is frozen in ice. Hell is to have your heart frozen.

Remember—if you are old enough—the mother, played by Mary Tyler Moore, in the film *Ordinary People?* Her two sons go sailing and get caught in a storm. The older one dies, but the young one survives. The mother cannot weep with her surviving son over their loss, and so she walls herself in a living tomb. She freezes her heart so it will not hurt. She cannot *Look*—and she cannot *Weep*—so she cannot *Live.*

Blessed are those who weep, for they will be comforted. And our comfort is that our Lord weeps with us. He doesn't take away our pain. He takes away our loneliness.

A mother said that one night she was very distressed. She had received some bad news about something. So she was sitting on her bed crying, and her seven-year-old daughter walked in holding a bowl of popcorn. The girl sat beside her mother and began wiping her face with kernels of popcorn and then eating them. That's us. We are the people that eat bread that is broken.

The desert fathers say it most clearly, "Weep, there is no other way." Our tears are the waters of baptism. Our tears are the water from a mother's womb that signals new life. Our tears are the spit Jesus rubs in people's eyes to cure their blindness. They come from the water table of the earth. The Eastern Orthodox say that tears are a gift of the Holy Spirit. They are a charism as valued as speaking in tongues or prophecy or healing. Weep, there is no other way.

And here's the good news: love brings life out of death. If we are willing to go to the cross and not run away to weep at the tomb, then love brings forth resurrected life.

Jesus cries out in a loud voice, *"Lazarus, come out!"* And he comes. He comes bound in strips of cloth. He comes out looking like Lon Chaney in the *Mummy.* Do you know why? It's not because Jesus is a magician. It's not because he knows the right words or waves some secret wand.

Lazarus comes out because he hears the voice of love calling him. Maybe this story is not about something Jesus does *to* Lazarus, but something Jesus does *with* Lazarus, as Barbara Brown Taylor writes in *God in Pain.* Love is what calls us out of death into new life. When Dante finds himself in the dark wood where the straight way was lost, the love of Beatrice and his love for her is what pulls him through his journey.

When we face death and weep our common loss, then we can find the love that saves us, because then we are honest about who we are and where we are and what we need. We know that we cannot save ourselves, but our communion with God in Christ—which we find in other people—brings us out of the tomb into the light.

The love which makes us weep is the very love that saves. We weep to open our hearts so we can receive the love that God is always giving us. Love brings us into resurrection—new life—different life. We don't go back to square one but to a different place. And it doesn't have to be as dramatic as the scene with Lazarus. In fact, I'm not sure it's such a good idea to go to someone's house and bellow, *"COME OUT!"*

Frederick Buechner tells about a time in his life when he was in a deep depression. At the time he was living in Vermont. One of his children was quite sick and his anxiety and worry over her finally was overwhelming. It was as if it had trapped him in a dark tomb.

One day the phone rang. It was a man from Charlotte, North Carolina, but he wasn't in Charlotte. He was just down the street from Buechner's house in Vermont. He had heard Buechner was in a bad place and thought "maybe it would be handy to have an extra friend around for a day or two." So he drove 800 miles.

Buechner says, "We just took a couple of walks, had a meal or two together and smoked our pipes, drove around some of the countryside, and that was about it . . . [but] I believe that for a little time we both of us touched the hem of Christ's garment, where both of us, for a little time anyway, were healed."[10]

Look—Weep—Live.

To look at where we are. To admit what parts of our life are dead. To see in what ways we have crawled into the tomb to weep over our losses. To join the community of tears so that we can console and be consoled. And then to hear the voice of Christ calling through all the voices of those who love us. To hear the voice that calls us to *Come out*. And then to have the grace and courage to step out into the light, so that like Lazarus—we, too, can be unbound and live.

---

10. Frederick Buechner, *Listening to Your Life*, (New York: HarperSanFrancisco, 1992), 311.

Contagious Love

 Micah 6:8; Psalm 80 or 80:1–7; Hebrews 10:5–10; Luke 1:39–49 (50–56)

When Elizabeth heard Mary's greeting, the child leaped in her womb.
Luke 1:41

This morning we moved a little closer to Christmas: no John the Baptist with his words of repentance and denunciations of that "brood of vipers." No dire warnings from Micah or the Book of Revelation. This morning we get the story of the visitation. Mary visits her relative, Elizabeth, to share her news. It's a story about God's love, about the power of that love.

This story teaches three lessons about that love.

First, love is contagious.

When something happens—when something amazing happens—what's the first thing you do?

You pick up the phone and call someone: *"Mom—I can't believe it! I just won the Lottery!"*

Or, *"I got a job"*— *"I'm getting married"*— *"the kids cleaned their rooms."* Or, whatever. . . .

Good news can't be bottled up. As soon as it gets inside us, it explodes. It pours out. It quakes inside us and demands to be shared. And it changes how we look at the world.

Mary has just had a visit from the Angel Gabriel. He has given her the astonishing news. Yes, Mary is not yet married. Yes, Mary is a virgin. Yes, she is very young. But she will give birth to the Messiah.

Luke tells us that as soon as Mary hears, she "went with haste" to see Elizabeth, her relative. Mary goes in haste to see Elizabeth because she is the only person who can appreciate her news.

Mary and Elizabeth are bookends. Neither expects what is happening to them. Mary is only about fourteen years old and Elizabeth is an old woman. Yet both are pregnant—both have been swept up in what God is doing in the world. Both have had their lives turned inside out by God.

So Mary goes to share her good news. She goes because if she doesn't let it out, she'll burst. She goes in haste. Now, Mary knows that Elizabeth is also pregnant because Gabriel has told her, but Elizabeth doesn't know about Mary. She is surprised to see her. Luke tells us:

> *When Elizabeth heard Mary's greeting, the child leaped in her womb.*

Love is contagious. It spreads from Mary to Elizabeth. The new life in Mary brings out the new life in Elizabeth. It's why we like being around people in love; we catch love from them.

Second, love is transformative. When the child leaped in Elizabeth's womb, she is changed. Not because she is aware of being pregnant, but because she has new sight. Elizabeth sees Mary in a new way. Luke says:

> *[Elizabeth] exclaimed with a loud cry, . . . "Why has this happened to me, that the mother of my Lord comes to me?"*

No longer is Mary her fourteen-year-old, unmarried, virgin cousin. No longer is Mary a woman who could be stoned under the laws of the Holiness Code. Elizabeth sees her as the Mother of her Lord—the Madonna.

The good news gets inside us and causes a fundamental revision. We see ourselves, and we see others completely differently. Our common calling is to be saints, and the chief characteristic of saints is not that they do good works. The chief characteristic is that they see the Christ in others. They know that each of us—teachers, salespersons, nurses—each of us is a Christ-bearer. We catch God's love from someone, and we never see the world the same again.

The fourteen-year-old virgin is the Madonna. And ordinary people like you and me have Christ inside us.

Love is contagious.

Love is transformative.

Third, love is not personal—it connects us to God's kingdom.

So often we think that love is a private feeling. It's about our private experience. But love—all true love—is bigger than that. When we know in our hearts that God loves us, that we are in Christ. When we feel God's blessing as Mary feels it, then the walls that separate our lives become permeable. I am part of you and you are part of me. Your pain is my pain; my joy is your joy. As John Donne says, "No man is an island."

Therefore, if you accept Jesus as your savior, you must *do justice, love kindness, and walk humbly with your God.* To be in love with the Christ is to feed the hungry and clothe the naked and shelter the homeless. Love is not personal. It connects us to the kingdom.

Mary comes and touches Elizabeth. And then the good news rebounds back to Mary and she breaks out in song. Suddenly the good news is bigger than the two of them. Suddenly it's about men and women neither woman has ever known. Mary knows that if God is breaking out in her and breaking out in Elizabeth, then God will break out beyond their lives and do surprising things for all people. God will lift up the lowly and fill the hungry with good things.

Once God's love is inside us, then we are compelled to be part of God's work in history. We cannot do otherwise. Dorothy Day didn't give food to the hungry because it was her duty. She did so because she had been embraced by the love of Christ. Mary and Elizabeth may seem a long way away from us. We may not really identify with either of these women. We may not like to think about being pregnant at fourteen or in our old age or at all.

But let's look again: The birth of Christ is not something that only happened 2000 years ago. We are not historians here gathering around to remember an event. We are here because the living Christ is inside each of us ready to give birth. Each of us probably feels as if we are like Elizabeth, unable to conceive, unable to bring life into the world. We may feel as if our life is already set. There are no surprises in store, at least no pleasant surprises.

But let us remember that *God so loved the world* that God brings about amazing surprises. *God so loved the world* that God is bringing the divine love into the world.

Let us remember—*that love is contagious—that love is transformative— that love connects us to the kingdom.*

Who knows? Maybe you'll talk to a relative over Christmas. Maybe some cousin or brother or sister will visit. Maybe someone will call and say, "You'll never guess what happened to me!"

And before you can reply, something will leap within you. And your life and the world will never be the same.

The Painful Plumb Line

 AMOS 7:7–15; PSALM 85 OR 85:7–13; EPHESIANS
1:1–14; MARK 6:7–14

*Then the Lord said, "See, I am setting a plumb line in the
midst of my people Israel."*
AMOS 7:8

Prophets are such pains—they just refuse to get with the program. Just
when things are going smoothly, they start making waves.

Today we heard from Amos. What a *pain* Amos was. Amos lived in
the good times of Israel. Jeroboam II is a powerful king. Israel is at
peace with her neighbors. The economy is good. People are working.
Life is humming along. Things are looking good and along comes
Amos. What *is* his problem? Why can't he get with the program?

Amos's problem is that God has given him a vision, and he cannot
get God's vision out of his head. Amos would like to get with the program. He'd like to go back to his sheep and sycamore trees. But he can't.

He can't because he no longer sees the world the way he used to.
God has shown him how out of kilter Israel is: *"See, I am setting a plumb
line in the midst of my people Israel."*

A *plumb line* is a reference point, a way of seeing how our ways are
different from God's ways. Prophets give us a way of standing back and
appraising our condition.

Our house in Nashville was built in 1924. So nothing was plumb.
You could put a marble in the center of any floor and it would roll to
the corner. So we were constantly in need of a level, an outside authority, because if we only looked at our environment, everything would
look right, but nothing would really be right.

Amos tells us he is a dresser of sycamore trees. That means he cuts
the top of the fruit open. If the fruit is healthy, letting air in makes it
ripen sooner and become juicier. If there are insects inside, opening it
up gets them out.

Amos is dressing Israel, cutting her open to show what is healthy
and what is not—and what does he find? Underneath the prosperity

and lack of conflict is a people who have forgotten God's command: to care for the poor, the defenseless, the little ones of the world. Amos says the law courts only serve the rich. Wealthy merchants were only concerned with their profit, and so they exploited the poor.

> *"They trample the heads of the weak into the dust of the earth and they force the lowly away."* (Amos 8:4)

The temples, he says, are only going through the motions, putting on better and better rituals but not changing people's hearts or their actions. Amos, like all prophets, is a pain because he calls us to account.

Well, what about us? What about our world? How does it look when we put it beside Jesus' plumb line?

Our first temptation is to focus on rules of behavior and sins of the flesh, and we could talk about promiscuity or adultery or sex outside marriage. Or, I always want to rail against violence and the abundance of guns. Or, we could go for alcohol and drug abuse. All those are sinful. All of those lead us away from God's ways. But I think Amos points us deeper. Amos points us to assumptions we make that are so insidious because they are so hidden. Let me try to get at this with a story:

> Once a woman went into a café. She sat at a table for two and ordered coffee and prepared to eat some cookies she had in her purse. The café was crowded, so a man took the other chair and also ordered coffee. The woman began reading her newspaper and then she reached over and took a cookie. She noticed the man took a cookie as well. This upset her, but she kept on reading.
>
> After a while she took another cookie, and so did he. She became angry and glared at the man. While she glared, he reached over and took the last cookie in the package and smiled and offered her half of it. The woman was indignant and left in a huff. As she was paying for her coffee, she noticed that in her purse was her package of unopened cookies.

Let me take this story and mention three hidden sins:

First, we worship things and we worship people who have things. We talk about obeying the Ten Commandments. But what about the Eighth Commandment: thou shalt not covet? Our economy is driven by creating desire. Although we have benefited greatly from our economic system, its downside is that it makes us want beyond our needs. Why do we need so many things when there are so many who have no things? Like the woman, we fixate on who owns what instead of sharing what lies before us. We forget that everything is given to us by God. And so we think we are entitled to these things.

Second, we are so afraid of one another. We think in terms of lawsuits, or being harmed, or being offended. I am all for making people accountable for their behavior, but we are called to see others as children of God—as brothers and sisters and not as threats. We know how to be "wise as serpents"; but what about "innocent as doves"? Like the woman—we don't think there's enough things or love or community. So we are fearful that those next to us will take what we have. We forget that Christ is found in community.

Finally, we have forgotten our call to sacrifice. What if those cookies really were the woman's? Why not take bread, bless it, break it, and share it? As Christians, we are commanded to love our neighbor in place of ourselves. I don't expect our society to talk about giving up for others, but I expect Christians to. I expect myself to. How often I fail. How often we fail.

The worship of things. The fear of others. The failure to sacrifice. My guess is that if Amos were here today, he might point to these sins and call us to repentance.

We gather together to remember that Jesus Christ is our plumb line. We ask God to help us be like the man in the café, the one who takes what by God's grace is given to him and shares it with others. So that Christ might join both of them at the table.

You Are My Beloved

The Baptism of our Lord

 ISAIAH 42:1–9; PSALM 72; ACTS 10:34–38;
LUKE 3:15–22

> *And the Holy Spirit descended upon him in bodily form like a*
> *dove. And a voice came from heaven, "You are my Son, the*
> *Beloved; with you I am well pleased."*
> LUKE 3:22

The Sunday after the Feast of the Epiphany is always the Baptism of our Lord. On this day we hear one of the gospel accounts of Jesus' baptism. Because this is Year C, today we hear Luke's version.

While Luke is my favorite gospel, I have to say today's passage feels like reading a bad translation. Luke gets all the right parts. There's water, and Jesus is baptized.

The heavens open and God announces that Jesus is "the Beloved." But the story really isn't much of a story.

Listen to it again.

> *Now when all the people were baptized, and when Jesus also had*
> *been baptized and was praying, the heaven was opened. . . . And*
> *a voice came from heaven, "You are my Son, the Beloved, with you*
> *I am well pleased."*

Luke, frankly, has no flare for the dramatic. Matthew puts Jesus and John the Baptist in the middle of the Jordan River. In Matthew's version, just as Jesus comes out of the water, the heavens part. And Charlton Heston's voice booms out with the words of God's blessing. But Luke just says:

> *And when Jesus also had been baptized and was praying, the*
> *heaven was opened. . . . And a voice came from heaven, "You are*
> *my Son, the Beloved; with you I am well pleased."*

In Luke's version, Jesus walks away from the crowds to pray presumably by himself. Here God addresses him alone instead of the crowd. In Matthew God speaks to the crowd and says: *This* is my Son, the Beloved. But in Luke God speaks to Jesus and says: *You are my Son, the Beloved.*

I have been reading this passage all week. Finally I realized that Luke is saying something slightly different from Matthew. Instead of focusing on how the crowd knows that Jesus is the beloved, Luke shows us a way to discover that through Jesus we too share in being God's beloved. The way is prayer. *Jesus was praying when the heavens opened.*

Prayer is the essential act for understanding who we are as God's beloved. The grace is given in baptism, but prayer is the means by which we live into it. Maybe that's why Luke's account of the baptism is not very dramatic—because the main activity happens in the connection between Jesus and God in prayer.

We know that Jesus is always praying in Luke's gospel. He goes to the mountain to pray before calling the disciples. He is praying alone just before Peter's confession that he is the Christ. He is praying on the mountain just before the Transfiguration. He is praying just before he gives the disciples the Lord's Prayer. And of course, he is praying at the Mount of Olives just before his arrest. Prayer is the air that Jesus breathes to stay alive.

And it is the air we must breathe if we are be fully alive in Christ. Without prayer, we just go from one experience to another never fully embracing it. Never really taking it in. Poet T. S. Eliot says *"We had the experience but missed the meaning."* Without prayer we too miss the meaning.

Maya Angelou says that when she was twenty-four, one of her professors asked her to read aloud a passage from *Love and Truth* that ends with *"God loves me."* She read it and closed the book and he said, *"Read it again."* She did so but in a sarcastic voice, and he said *"Read it again."* After about the seventh time of reading the passage she says:

> *I began to sense that there might be truth in the statement that God really did love me. Me. Maya Angelou. I suddenly began to cry at the grandness of it all.*[11]

11. Maya Angelou, *Wouldn't Take Nothing for My Journey Now* (New York: Random House, 1993).

That's what prayer does. It makes us slow down and ponder the simple mysteries of grace until the reality of God's love permeates into all of our being. Jesus was baptized and then he prayed—he let the reality of that into his heart and soul. Then he heard the words of grace— *God loves me.*

So what is prayer? Let's first acknowledge that there are various kinds of prayer. When we normally think of prayer, we think primarily of *intercessory prayer:* As with our Prayers of the People where we hold up to God those whom we love. *"Dear Lord,"* we say *"remember these people in their sorrow and in their joy."*

Of course we have prayers of *thanksgiving*—prayers of *praise.* That's what most of the opening part of our worship is—*Blessed be God* we say. *Glory to God in the highest*—we sing. And the list goes on—prayers of *petition*, prayers of *oblation*, prayers of *penitence*, and so on.

However, the crucial kind of prayer is what the Prayer Book calls *"Adoration"* but most of us know as "Contemplative Prayer." The Prayer Book defines this prayer as *"lifting up of the heart and mind to God, asking nothing but to enjoy God's presence."*

Contemplative Prayer is not us telling God anything. It's not our doing anything or calling on God to do anything about the world or those we love. It's simply being open to experiencing the presence of God inside you—all around you.

Jesus was baptized—presumably by John—in the Jordan River. No doubt that act was important. But then he went to pray. And it was in prayer that the heavens opened and God told Jesus—*You are my Beloved.* At that moment Jesus received all the grace he would ever need. If you hear God saying deep in your heart and soul *"I am well pleased with you,"* you receive the peace the world cannot give and the world cannot take away.

It is clear in Luke's gospel that Jesus returns to remember those words at the crucial junctures in his ministry. In the blur of everyday life, it is so easy to get caught up in the ways of the world, that we forget who we are. Unless we take time to pray—to stop and let the mystery sink all the way into our souls.

If we don't stop and pray we will never receive the transformative power of the sacraments or of God's love. If we don't pray, then of course we can go through the motions of worship, go through the motions of being baptized or receiving the body and blood or being alive, and never hear God whispering that we are the beloved.

On this Feast of the Baptism of our Lord, it is well to remember that baptism is about identity. Whenever we baptize an infant, I say to the parents *"Name this child."*

Because baptism is where we receive our true name—not just our Christian name—*Granville Porter,* but the beloved—*the one with whom God is well pleased*—that's our true name. The truth is God is always saying those words. In every moment of our lives, God is whispering in our hearts and souls. Remember you are my *beloved*—*the one with whom I am well pleased.*

It's just that we are so distracted, we can't hear it. It's as if we live in a world of amnesia. Prayer is the cure to amnesia. We are all called to go deep within to remember who we are and what we have been given in our own baptism. Wherever we were baptized, we went into the waters of the Jordan River. And God said to us *You are my beloved—the one with whom I am well pleased.*

In baptism, we are made Christ's own forever—so what else is it that we need? We run around like the scarecrow, lion, and tin man looking for certificates to give us what we already have. We don't need anything that the any wizard has. We just need to remember who we are and to do what our Lord did all the time—pray.

There's an old *Simpsons'* episode where Lisa's favorite teacher is leaving her school and moving to another city. Lisa is distraught. On his last day the teacher says to her, *"Lisa, whenever you feel sad or unhappy or abandoned, I want you to remember 4 words: "I am Lisa Simpson."*

That is our task as well. To remember *I am baptized; therefore I am God's beloved. And God is well pleased with me.*

To Dream As God Dreams

Sermons of Hope

Holy Fools

MICAH 6:1–8; PSALM 37:1–18 OR 37:1–6;
I CORINTHIANS 1:(18–25) 26–31; MATTHEW 5:1–12

But God chose what is foolish in the world to shame the wise.
I CORINTHIANS 1:27

Coming from the small town of Asheville, North Carolina, my eyes were opened in many ways when I went to the University of North Carolina. I met many people who were very different from me, people from different places. Some richer, some poorer, but none was as different as Greg Carver.

At first, our differences were small. He was from Philadelphia. He was Roman Catholic. He was about a foot shorter than I was. But the differences grew. Greg moved out of the dorm and started living in a tree house in the woods. He started the Polar Bears Club: a group that went swimming in the lake on the last day of exams in December. When my sister and I turned twenty-one, Greg organized a parade down Chapel Hill's main street. (Of course, the police had no advance warning of this.)

And when Greg came to my wedding, he wore no shoes. At that event, my new father-in-law pulled me aside, pointed to Greg, and asked, "Is he for real?"

It's only recently that I have found the right category for Greg. He's a fool. Not a fool in the sense of being stupid but a fool like a jester. Fools are the persons on the edge of our society who remind us that our practicality has a cost. The jester is the one who keeps the king or queen honest and humble.

The problem is that we don't know what to do with the fool. *Is he for real?* is another way of saying: *Wait until you get into the real world.* And by *real world* we mean the one that has the goals of *security, prestige, and autonomy.* To be safe, to be important, to be unencumbered.

The hard edge of the gospel is that we are called to be fools for Christ. The good news of Jesus Christ is always foolish to the world. As

Paul says, it is always *folly* and a *stumbling block*. The world cannot make sense of Jesus. His notion of blessedness seems upside down.

So instead of *Blessed are the meek*—*Blessed are the power players.*

So instead of *Blessed are the persecuted*—*Blessed are the protected.*

So instead of *Blessed are those who mourn*—*Blessed are the detached.*

In the first century, there was a crucifix with Jesus having the head of an ass—not to be irreverent, but to remind the viewers that Jesus invites us into the foolishness of the gospel. For the gospel is a world right-side-up that appears upside-down. Our Lord speaks folly: losing is finding; the last are the first; the weak are strong; dying is living. These things all appear foolish.

Before I was called to St. Gregory, I interviewed with a parish in Washington, DC. It was a very liberal, affluent, progressive place, filled with "important" people. During one of the question/answer periods, one lady asked me about my vision of the church.

And I said, *"It's where the broken people of the world find hope and redemption."*

She blurted out—*"We don't have broken people here."* This good news was too foolish for her.

So we are invited to be holy fools. We are invited to remember that being a holy fool is part of our tradition. Remember the Beatles' song, "Fool on the Hill"? Or *Godspell?* Our Lord is inviting us to step out of our seriousness, out of our properness, into the freedom of foolishness. He invites us to let our seriousness go and embrace the joy of the good news. He invites us to stop being life-killing Pharisees who are always "correct" but never alive.

We are invited to join the great history of fools for Christ: people like St. Simeon of Sulos, who in the sixth century used to throw nuts at the candles during the liturgy, just to dispel the deadly seriousness of the mass.

Or, of course, St. Francis, who elevated holy foolishness to new heights. He gave away all his possessions. He walked to the Holy Land to ask the sultan to stop fighting the crusaders. Francis used to stand on his head so he could see the world right-side-up. And he called for his friars to be jesters—jokers—so they could appreciate the joy of grace.

And we have contemporary fools, like the man in Tiananmen Square who faced down the tanks.

Or Lenny Skutnik who jumped into the Potomac River to save a drowning woman in midwinter. The fools are people who give their time, their money, their lives to help others. They are ordinary folks like you and me, who know that dying to the self is gaining life with Christ.

But it remains hard to be a fool. It doesn't come easy to us. Most of us want what the world wants: security—prestige—autonomy. In 1973 my father lost his job. He was vice president of a sweater company. The country went through a depression, and people no longer could afford cashmere sweaters. So in one fell swoop, he lost all that the world says is important. He no longer had security—prestige—autonomy. But even though it seemed like a great curse, I think it was a great gift to him and to our family, because it taught us a little bit about holy foolishness.

My mother and father moved to a farm and suddenly my father could do all the things he always wanted to do. So he started collecting animals: goats and pigs and ponies and parakeets and dogs. He no longer had to live the life of the world, so he was invited to live—to live fully.

Sometimes that's what it takes. We have to be forced into accepting the foolishness of the gospel:

Dying is living.

The last are first.

Giving is receiving.

For Christianity is like a good joke; either you get it, or you don't. The joke is that the cross is the door to life. The more our safe, inflated, private ego dies, the more we find Christ in us.

The joke is that death always leads to life. Remember *Dead Man Walking?* The convicted man just before he is executed says, "I didn't know I had to die to love." The joke is that God so loves us that God sent his Son into the world so that we might become like him.

I haven't seen Greg Carver since 1972. I heard he is a piano tuner in Boston. While I hope he doesn't still live in a tree house or jump into the Boston Harbor in December, I hope he is still a fool. I hope that every now and then when he goes somewhere to tune a piano, somewhere important like the Boston Symphony Hall, that once in a while he doesn't wear his shoes.

Saying "Yes" in a Time of "No"

 GENESIS 15:1–12, 17–18; PSALM 27; PHILIPPIANS 3:17–4:1; LUKE 13:(22–30) 31–35

> [The Lord] brought [Abram] outside and said, "Look toward heaven and count the stars, if you are able to count them."
> Then he said to him, "So shall your descendants be."
> GENESIS 15:5

In the afternoon of the day and in the afternoon of our lives, we begin to think about what might have been. Those dreams we thought we had put on the shelf a long time ago come tumbling down and possess us once more. We gaze into the gathering twilight and say to ourselves: "I never thought my life would be like *this*. In spite of it all, I always hoped I'd—be a ballerina—or live at the ocean—or get married—or go to law school." Or—whatever it is.

In the afternoon of the day and in the afternoon of our lives, we don't know what to do with all those hopes and dreams of our youth. We find ourselves admitting that "I'm not going to play for the Boston Celtics, or be a millionaire, or have grandkids, or. . . ." We gaze into the gathering twilight and wonder what happened to what-might-have-been.

Our usual response is to cope with our loss. We learn to live with the emptiness of those dreams that never came to pass. We say to ourselves: "It's okay—it all worked out for the best." And maybe it is okay, but it is only okay as long as our dreams really are small.

I always wanted to be the next Elvis. When I was in the third grade, I used Vitalis on my hair and I practiced sneering in the mirror. I was certain someone would discover me and whisk me off to wherever it is you get whisked off to when you become famous. Even in the third grade I knew I couldn't sing, but I still dreamed.

I dreamed until I grew up and learned about how the world worked. And then that dream faded away. Now, to be honest, one reason the dream faded away is that I really didn't want to sing. I just wanted to be famous. So the dream wasn't really founded on my true self. It wasn't really a dream; it was a wish.

But what about the dreams that are real dreams—true callings from God that come from our hearts? What about dreams that are not just fantasies about our own ego? What do we do with them in the late afternoon? Well, if we are as lucky as Abraham (Abram), the late afternoon of our lives is when we learn about faith. Instead of going from dreaming to despair, we go from dreaming to hope.

Abraham and Sarah are in old age, and yet their dreams are still young. They dream of something new being born. They want to pass themselves on to the next generation. They want a son and land. They do want to be rooted in something bigger than themselves. And they have held onto this dream for a long time, well past their childbearing years.

The Lord comes, and Abraham hears the promise out of the Lord's mouth: *"Don't be afraid, Abram—I haven't forgotten you and Sarah—remember the promise: Land—don't worry."*

"But," Abraham replies, *"even if I had land, I don't have any sons. Do I have to leave the land to my slave?"*

"Don't be afraid. You shall have a son. Wait, I'll show you. Look at the stars. You'll have more kids and grandkids and great-great-great grandkids than stars in the sky."

Abraham felt God embracing him, and Abraham believed. He moved to a place beyond reason and logic, a place called faith. Faith is the place between the promises and our own sense of barrenness. In that place we do not deny the darkness of the present, but we live in expectation of the light. We know where we are, but we are filled with hope. Hope is not about a designated future. Hope doesn't say, *"If I am good and do my duty, I will get exactly what I asked for."* If I just use Vitalis and sneer enough, I'll be Elvis.

God is not Santa Claus. We're not sitting on his lap and giving him our list. Faith is not about cutting a deal: "I'll believe if you give me the sons." Faith is when we are overwhelmed by the presence of God, so we know that we are held by something bigger than ourselves. We participate in the arc of salvation. We are part of the divine plan that is bringing in the kingdom in the midst of barrenness.

Our faith is not in ourselves but in God. Abraham believed in the Lord, not in some carefully laid-out strategy. Abraham fell in love with God; Abraham wanted to align his life with God's activity in the world. When Abraham asks for some assurance, God doesn't call in a fertility expert to explain how Abraham and Sarah are going to get pregnant. God doesn't turn into a real estate agent. God says, *"I am the Lord—the one who makes promises. I am asking you to embrace my promises, to base your life on them."*

Like you and me, Abraham lived in a time when the world seemed to say *"No"* to all he desired. No kids—no land—no dreams. And God came and said what God always says: *"In a time of 'No,' I am asking you to say 'Yes.'"*

Faith is saying *"Yes"* in a world of *"No."*

So here we are, not so far from Abraham, filled with dreams of a future we fear will never happen. As T. S. Eliot says, *"Between the idea and reality falls the shadow."* The shadow is that fearful voice that accepts the *"No"* of the world. Walter Brueggemann says that fearful voice is what makes us sane and sober and prudent and competent, but it also drives us to despair, fatigue, cynicism, and even brutality.

To get away from the *"No"* of the world to the *"Yes"* of God, we must change our focus from ourselves to God. We will never embrace the new life that God intends so long as we stare at our barrenness. The Bible never uses the word *create* with a human subject. Human beings *make* or *form,* but only God *creates*—only God brings about a new thing.

So long as we think about our own capacities, our dreams will always be small. We will be stuck in the *"No"* of the world. God calls us to shift our vision from ourselves to God. Then we can believe the promises—then we can say *"Yes"* in the midst of *"No."*

God asks for us to look up from ourselves to the stars, to the divine pattern. Then God asks us to hope wildly:

Can you imagine having a son? Land? Descendants more numerous than the stars?

Can you imagine the blind seeing because a rabbi touches them? The deaf hearing, the dead being raised?

Can you imagine new life for yourself?

Your barrenness bringing abundant life?

Can you imagine a world of justice and mercy and peace?

Can you say *"Yes"* to God in a world of *"No"*?

We don't get the end of the story today, but we know the rest. Abraham and Sarah say *"Yes."* And Isaac is born, whose name means *laughter.* Because when we say *"Yes,"* then even in a barren world of *"No"*—then we are able to throw our heads back and laugh. Because God has let us in on the divine joke: Despite the way the world looks, all the promises—are true.

Carried by Friends

Isaiah 43:18–25; Psalm 32 or 32:1–8;
2 Corinthians 1:18–22; Mark 2:1–12

> *Then some people came, bringing to him a paralyzed man,
> carried by four of them.*
> Mark 2:3

When the four friends first came to see him, he didn't want to hear what
they had to say: *"You guys have been drinking, haven't you? Let me get this right.
You plan on carrying me from our town all the way to Capernaum so we can see
a healer, a person you've never met? Is that it?"*

The hope of walking no longer gave him anything but pain—and
disappointment. So he had put it aside a long time ago. He had come
to accept being paralyzed. It was just the way it was. All this talk about
a healer opened a door he had shut. But there were four of them and
one of him. And they were so excited.

*"Jonathan, think about it. You can walk. We can go dancing. It will be like old
times again. We want you to try. We know that this is the one!*

"Do it for us. We'll carry you. Do it for yourself!" They sounded like
children asking for ice cream: *"Please—Oh, Please."*

And so they went. The trip was bad enough, but then Capernaum
was a zoo. Jonathan didn't expect anyone else to be there. After all, who
would be as nuts as his friends were? But when they got to the house
where this healer was, it was mobbed. People were standing in the street.
One person couldn't squeeze through the crowd, much less four people
carrying a stretcher.

"Okay," he said. *"We tried. Let's go get something to eat and get out of here."*

"Are you out of your mind," they screamed. *"You are going to walk."*

So they went around the block, looking for a back door. But all they
found was a ladder to the roof.

"Guys, I don't do ladders. Remember?" But they tied him down on a
board, and up he went, as if that would get them anywhere, he thought.

This is when things got really crazy. David, Jonathan's best friend,
leaned down to Jonathan's face and whispered: *"I want you to walk, and*

I am going to get you to this healer, even if it breaks both your legs." With that, David took an ax and started chopping through the roof. And they lowered him down.

He felt wholly dependent on his friends. He couldn't see where he was going. All he could see was his friends' faces above in the hole in the roof. When his stretcher touched the floor, the crowd had backed away. There was just the stranger, the healer who looked down at him.

"My friends believe you can help," Jonathan said.

The stranger looked up toward the hole in the roof and said, *"When I see your friends' faces, I see the face of faith."*

Looking back down, he said to Jonathan: *"Child, your sins are forgiven. Stand up and walk."*

What an outrageous story this is! Maybe because it's in the Bible we don't realize its outrageousness. It violates our sense of private property—after all, they do make a hole in the roof. But most of all it violates our sense of individualism, our love of the solitary hero.

One of my favorite films is *High Noon.* Gary Cooper, the lone stranger, rides into town and faces down the bad guys by himself. Bruce Willis in *Die Hard*—Sylvester Stallone in *Rambo.* There is something appealing about thinking of ourselves as rugged individualists, working out our own salvation, pulling ourselves up by our own bootstraps.

One on one with God. But there is a reason Batman has Robin, and the Lone Ranger has Tonto, and Don Quixote has Sancho Panza. As appealing as Gary Cooper is, sometimes we find ourselves paralyzed. We are unable to move our feet. We are cut off from the animating life force, and parts of ourselves are frozen. And we need someone to carry us to the source of life. The truth is that we are interconnected. I need you and you need me. It's what we call the body of Christ. My life is part of your life and your life is part of mine. We are "companions" on the way: "com"+ "pan"= "eating bread together."

The story today is about Jesus' ability to heal and to forgive sins. It is also about how the scribes are so hung up on the rules of religion that they miss the point.

But it is also about the importance of companionship. In a few moments, we will baptize Emily into the body of Christ. Her life will become part of our life. Her parents and godparents will make promises that they will try to help her avoid paralysis. But they are also promising to be there for her when she becomes paralyzed. And maybe they should think about this: They are promising, if it is necessary, to carry her on a stretcher from her house to St. Gregory and to take a chain saw to our roof.

However, we all need to think about it, because I will also ask all of you: *"Will you who witness these vows do all in your power to support this person in her life in Christ?"* I am asking you if you will carry her. I am asking you if when she is in need, you will cast aside your embarrassment and your need to obey the rules and take desperate measures. Are you willing to chainsaw your way through whatever separates your friends from the source of life?

Emily is going to need you, just as you and I need one another. We need each other for advice and comfort and chicken soup. But we also need one another to remind us of who we are.

The man became so paralyzed that he forgot he was worth saving. He forgot that as a child of God, he, too, deserved to be by the side of Jesus Christ. So he gave up on himself. He said to himself, *"It's too far. There are too many people. I can't get there. He couldn't help me anyway."*

Companions are those who remember our true self even when we forget it. Companions are those who refuse to give up on us even when we give up on ourselves. They see something in us that we had forgotten was there. So the paralyzed man's friends say to him: *"You are worth the journey. You are worth the lawsuits we are going to have to face for tearing up this guy's house. You are worth all the trouble because we remember who you are. We know that you are more than your paralysis. Our love for you is stronger than your frozen state."*

Jesus wants us to be companions like that. That's why Mark writes: *"When Jesus saw their faith, he said to the paralytic. . . ."*

Jesus doesn't heal the paralytic because of his faith but because of his friends' faith. Friends remind us of the best parts of ourselves that we had forgotten.

When I get low and blue, sometimes I call one of my friends. I don't have anything really important to say. I don't want him to fix my problems, I just want to hear his voice. I want him to remind me that someone loves me, that someone somewhere thinks I am important enough to saw a hole in a roof if that's what it takes to help me out.

That's why every week we pray for one another. We share our hopes and our fears with one another. Sometimes we feel so low, we can't even pray for ourselves—we need someone else.

Remember the film or the novel, *The Natural?* Roy Hobbs, who is a baseball player and the hero, has been going through a horrible slump. The crowd has turned against him. He comes up to the plate, and everyone boos. Except one woman who has loved him since he was a teenager. When he comes to the plate, she stands up. Roy looks at her, and he knows that she remembers who he truly is. And his slump ends.

In baptism we are made part of the body of Christ. That means that we are going to be Christ's eyes in this broken world. Whenever we see someone frozen, someone cut off from the source of life, we are to do whatever it takes. We are to love him or her outrageously. We are to come out of our private homes and lives and carry one another.

My guess is that after all the excitement died down, Jonathan and the four others started walking home. And they had their arms around one another partly because Jonathan hadn't walked in a long time, and partly because it felt right.

Finally Jonathan said: *"I don't know how to thank you, but I still can't believe you cut a hole in the roof."*

The four said, *"Hey, we're your friends. Wouldn't you do the same for us?"*

From Dragons to Children

ISAIAH 2:10–17; PSALM 89:1–18 OR 89:1–4, 15–18;
ROMANS 6:3–11; MATTHEW 10:34–42

> *Do you not know that all of us who have been baptized into*
> *Christ Jesus were baptized into his death? Therefore . . . just as*
> *Christ was raised from the dead by the glory of the Father, so*
> *we too might walk in newness of life.*
>
> ROMANS 6:3–4

In the third book of the *Narnia Chronicles*, C. S. Lewis tells the story of
Eustace: a self-centered boy who systematically isolates himself from
his companions and finds himself more and more alone and alienated.
Eustace wanders off by himself to an island where he discovers a dragon's lair and a treasure. But before he can steal any of it, he is turned
into a dragon himself. Eustace is no longer the boy God created him to
be. He is cut off from his true self and cut off from the human family. He is trapped in a dragon's skin.

Eustace is rescued by Aslan, the lion. Aslan leads him to a clear well
and tells Eustace to shake off his dragon scales. Eustace shakes off as
many as he can. Like a snake he sheds his skin three times. But he cannot get rid of his dragon skin by himself. So he lies down and the lion
comes over, and using his claws, tears into Eustace's skin.

Eustace says: *"The very first tear the lion made was so deep that I thought*
it had gone right into my heart. And when he began pulling the skin off, it hurt
worse that anything I ever felt.

"Well, he peeled the beastly stuff right off. . . . And there I was smooth and
soft as a peeled switch.

"Then he caught hold of me and threw me into the water. It smarted like any-
thing but only for a moment. After that it became perfectly delicious and . . .
I found that all the pain had gone.

"Then I saw why. I'd turned into a boy again."

How often do we become a dragon? Despite all we know, despite
all that those who love us try to tell us, we lose our way and find ourselves trapped in some cave, some dark lonely place; surrounded by all

the things we thought we wanted, but know only too late are worthless. In that lostness, we find that we have turned into something other than who we really are.

This is the condition St. Paul addresses in his letter to the Romans. He is writing to the Christians in Rome who have lost sight of who they are as disciples of Jesus Christ. They have mistaken the gospel of free grace for freedom to do whatever they want. So they have wandered from the straight path and to a dragon cave. St. Paul tells them and tells us: (1) what we must do; (2) how we must do it; and (3) what the end result will be.

What must we do?

"Do you not know that all of us who have been baptized into Christ Jesus were baptized into his death? . . . For if we have been united with him in a death like his, we will certainly be united with him in a resurrection like his."

Each time we lose our way, each time we find ourselves turned into the dragon of our false self, each time we allow our fears to drive us into that dark place, before we can be resurrected, we must die. We cannot walk in newness of life until we shed our old deadly ways. Like Eustace, we must shake off our dragon skin. That dragon skin is the part of us that keeps us from accepting God's grace. It keeps us from embracing the fact that we are a child of God. It keeps us from believing that God has brought us out of sin into righteousness; out of death into life.

The dragon skin is whatever entraps us—whatever binds us. It can take the form of addictions: addictions to food or alcohol or sex or work. Or it can be a low self-esteem, or hardness of heart, or fear of other people, or jealousy. Whatever it is, we must shed the dragon skin.

And it is hard. A professor at Emory, James Fowler, has written about stages in "faith development," and it seems very logical and orderly. But shedding the dragon skin is not about any kind of development. It's about death. It's about letting go of our old ways and facing the unknown.

I read somewhere that when Boris Yeltsin was baptized, the priest was drunk and he dropped Yeltsin into the baptismal pool and he almost drowned. The child was fished out alive. That's what must happen to all of us. We don't "almost drown"; we must drown.

As Paul says in Galatians, *"I have been crucified with Christ; and it is no longer I who live, but it is Christ who lives in me."*

Well, you are saying to yourself, *that's poetic; that's nice. But how do we die?* The truth is we cannot kill our dragons by ourselves. Eustace cannot shake off all the dragon scales. It takes Aslan to put Eustace's dragon self to death.

The twelve step community has discovered a central truth: we are powerless to cure ourselves. An alcoholic needs a higher power to get sober. And we need Jesus Christ to bring us through the waters of death into newness of life. We cannot baptize ourselves. Only another person representing Christ can do that. And we cannot get out of our caves by ourselves. We must ask God to remove our shortcomings. The promise is that when we do ask, God will respond. So we must finally give up on coping with dying. We must finally stop trying to put makeup over our dragon skin, look at who we have become, and ask God to deliver us.

That plea is the beginning of faith because that plea for deliverance means trusting that God will do for us what we cannot do for ourselves. God will bring us out of slavery through the waters of the Red Sea into the Promised Land.

In the Episcopal liturgy in the middle of the eucharistic prayers, the priest says, "We proclaim the mystery of faith: Christ has died. Christ is risen. Christ will come again." The mystery we proclaim is that death is always followed by resurrection.

On the other side of death is new life. If we die with Christ, we are resurrected with him. The resurrection is both totally new and totally familiar. It's like Mary Magdalene seeing the risen Christ—he looks like the gardener, yet he looks like her Lord. Or it's like Eustace—after he is thrown into the water, he doesn't turn into some alien person. He becomes a boy again; he becomes fully Eustace.

In baptism we are given our names. In so doing, God affirms the uniqueness of who we are, and joins us to the body of Christ. At thirty-six years of age, Tolstoy was thrown from his horse while hunting. When he came to his senses, a thought hit him like a thunderbolt— *"I am a writer."* Amid the pain from the fall, he felt tremendous joy. Right after that he began writing *War and Peace.* That fall, that near death, jarred him to his senses. So suddenly he knew who he was and what he wanted to do.

This new life is different, but it feels completely right because we are coming home to ourselves. We are living the life we were created to live. Of course, we are forgetful creatures. We will wander off again and again and think we are dragons only to be carried by Christ through the waters of death into new life, again and again and again. Each time, we remember a little more of who we are. Each time we claim a little more of our birthright. Death and resurrection is the pattern of our lives. It's the DNA of our souls. Eustace didn't become a saint. He became a little boy once more. And like all children and like all adults, Eustace will lose his way again.

He will sometimes be selfish and unkind. He will find himself in an alien land filled with dragons. But once we are thrown by the Lion Christ into the waters of baptism, somewhere deep inside us we know that our true name can never be taken away from us. However lost we feel, let us remember that God will help us kill off our dragon self. And God will lead us to the place called resurrection, which is the place where we are ourselves, and we are home.

Removing the Veil

 EZEKIEL 2:1–7; PSALM 123; II CORINTHIANS
12:2–10; MARK 6:1–6

*He left that place and came to his hometown. . . . And he
could do no deed of power there.*
MARK 6:1, 5

At this point in the story Jesus has been doing well. He's been healing
the sick and infirm. The crowds are growing and growing. And so he
decides it's time to go home.

So he comes to Nazareth: a small, obscure little town, a place not
even mentioned in the Hebrew Scriptures. Perhaps some of the disciples assume that the folks will be impressed. Finally someone from this
insignificant crossroads has made it big. Maybe there'll be a parade.
Maybe they'll name a street for Jesus. But no one shouts *"Hosanna."*

As Mark writes, *"He could do no deed of power there."* The people could
not see Jesus the Messiah, the miracle worker, the healer, the prophet.
They only saw Mary's boy, the illegitimate one. The carpenter who's
pretending to be a rabbi. For the people of Nazareth, their assumptions
about Jesus prevent them from seeing him as he is.

Now this is a typical situation: We know "You can't go home
again." It doesn't matter what you have done since you left your hometown, you'll always hear, "I knew you when you were only this high."
I know when I go to Asheville, North Carolina, where I grew up, I experience a sort of time warp when I drive past the city limits. And I have
this weird sense that I look as if I am sixteen years old.

But Mark is describing something bigger than just dealing with
our hometowns. He is describing the ways our interpretations, our
assumptions, make us blind to the grace that is all about us. We think
we know the way the world works, and because of those assumptions
we cannot see the Christ standing right in front of us. Jesus is ready
to bring his healing touch to Nazareth, but *"He could do no deed of
power there."* Because the people could not let go of their ways of seeing
him.

I heard a wonderful quote that I believe is from St. Augustine: *"You are the veil that separates you from the paradise you seek."* So often we assume that to get to the paradise we seek demands dramatic external change:

I need to go to California.

Or we as a society need to pass this law.

Now sometimes we do need to do these things. Sometimes we need to change the circumstances of the world, but sometimes the block is internal, not external. Sometimes the veil is inside us—we only see what we think we should see.

That cannot be the Messiah—it's only Mary's son.

Nothing miraculous can happen here—it's only Nazareth.

And so we can become cynical about our problems: There's nothing we can do about the violence in our cities. The cycle of poverty is too ingrained for us to change it. Racism is just too *deep to cure.*

Patrick White, the novelist, once said: *"There is another world, but it's the same as this one."* So often what we need is simply to change our vision, to open our eyes to see the grace that is in front of us, to see with the eyes of faith, to believe that God is always ready to transform our world.

We need one another, because left to ourselves we are capable of infinite self-deception. It's so easy to worship our experience of God instead of the living God. I help you be honest and you help me. When I say something stupid, you can tell me so. Wouldn't it have been wonderful if someone had challenged the people of Nazareth? What if someone had said, *"Well, yes, he is Mary's son—but close your eyes and touch him—and feel what happens"*?

We need one another for an additional reason: We need to remind one another of the story—*"Yes, I know he doesn't look like the Messiah, but, remember Jacob? Sometimes God chooses unlikely people."*

Let me end with a story. Once there was a man from Crete who loved his country very much. He loved Crete more than anything else. Just before his death, he grabbed a handful of Crete's dirt and clasped it to his breast. He came to the gates of heaven and St. Peter said, *"To enter you must let go of your handful of dirt."*

But the man refused. *"This is my country,"* he cried.

And so St. Peter went away and came back after 100 years. Again he told the man to let go of his dirt, and again he refused. Finally, after hundreds of years, the man let go his handful of Cretan soil and

St. Peter opened the gates. And before the man lay the Island of Crete.

"You are the veil that separates you from the paradise you seek."

God is always eager to usher us into paradise. In the face of every man and woman is the face of Jesus Christ. Let us let go of our presuppositions and remove the veil.

All the Way to Heaven

ECCLESIASTES 1:12–14, 2:(1–7, 11) 18–23;
PSALM 49 OR 49:1–11; COLOSSIANS 3:(5–11) 12–17;
LUKE 12:13–21

*I saw all the deeds that are done under the sun; and see, all is
vanity and a chasing after wind.*
ECCLESIASTES 1:14

Ecclesiastes is not a book for the young. In fact, you ought to have to
prove you are at least thirty-five years old before you are allowed to
read it.

You can't understand why this person is so negative until you are
middle-aged. When we are young, it won't make sense because we think
we can do anything and have anything and change everything. But then
we hit what the desert fathers call the "noonday devil."

It's because at noon, in the middle of our life, everything is in stark
clarity. We see where we are and what we are. We recognize that the
things we thought were so important—aren't: success, possessions,
positions of power, the trappings of our life.

As Richard Rohr says, we spend the first half of our life climbing
a ladder, but discover it's against the wrong wall. In the middle of our
life, we realize that we are mortal and we realize how fragile life is. Our
bodies don't work the way they should, nor do they look the way they
should. Last year I pulled a muscle in my leg playing basketball. And
my first thought was, this doesn't happen to me.

We could talk about losing hair or gray hair or weight distribution,
but we won't. In the middle of our life there just is this
gap between the way we thought the world would be and the way the
world is. Something happens to make us realize that we live in time.
Maybe our parents get sick or die. Maybe marriages fall apart; it could
be anything. We finally take it in that everything we thought would
last passes.

Everything we thought was forever fades away.

In the words of John Keats, when I face the fragility of life:

96

> *Then on the shore of the wide world I stand alone and think*
> *Till love and fame to nothingness do sink.*

That's why Ecclesiastes is not a book for the young. It only makes sense when there is as much time behind you as in front of you. Only then can we say what that writer says, "All is vanity." We work so hard, but for what? Nothing lasts; it all passes away. All is vanity.

Vanity is not a very good translation of the Hebrew word, *hebel*. Literally *hebel* means *breath* or *vapor. Hebel* refers to whatever exists in time, whatever is transitory, whatever lives and dies. Instead of *vanity* we might translate *hebel* as *time-bound* or even *mortal.* We like to believe that we live on solid ground or that we can make a permanent mark on the world, but *hebel* tells us that nothing lasts. Our lives are but a breath or vapor.

Ecclesiastes is not an uplifting book. It offers no way out of *hebel.* So long as we live "under the sun," we are victims of time. There is part of us that resists that, of course. So we try to defeat time. We try changing our appearance: face-lifts, hair dye, and on and on.

Or we try to defeat time by gathering possessions around us. There is a new ad out for Volkswagen: "If you sold your soul in the 80s, you can buy it back in the 90s—get a VW Beetle." Why do we continue to believe we can buy our souls?

Why do we believe salvation can be found in things? I saw in the paper that the new owner of O. J. Simpson's four-million-dollar mansion tore it down so he could rebuild it the way he wanted.

This is vanity. This is *hebel.*

We cannot change the fact of time. All of us age; all of us will die. But we can change our perspective.

In the letter to the Colossians, Paul says:

> *So if you have been raised with Christ, seek the things that are above, where Christ is, seated at the right hand of God. Set your minds on things that are above, not on things that are on earth.*

So long as we set our minds on things below, we are locked in time. We confront the finality of death, and all is vanity. We only see our lives as a small chronology between birth and death. But if we set our mind on things that are above, we see ourselves and lives through God's eyes. Then everything changes. All is vanity so long as we are the only actors in the drama of our lives. But from above, we are part of a larger pattern—a pattern of God renewing us, sustaining us, redeeming us. A pattern of death and resurrection—of discovering new life in places we thought were dead. That's why *hebel* is not the only breath in the New Testament. There is also *ruach*. *Ruach* is not a poof of air but the creative wind that blew upon the waters of creation.

Ruach is the prophetic wind that filled the prophets. *Ruach* is the renewing wind that constantly re-creates the world and its beings. *Ruach* is the Holy Spirit that blew on those in the Upper Room. This wind joins us to the eternal God when we are filled with it. If we only focus on our breath, we only discover *hebel*. The writer of Ecclesiastes calls *hebel* "a chasing after wind." The King James Version calls it a "vexation of the spirit."

Hebel is our attempt to capture *ruach* through our own efforts, but this is truly vanity. Yes, *hebel* is a part of our lives, but it is not the only part. There is also *ruach*.

Catherine of Siena said, "All the way to heaven is heaven." God's creative, sustaining, renewing breath is always blowing in our world. That breath gives us a taste here and now of what is promised in the next life. We cannot know it fully, but we can know that *hebel* vanishes like a vapor, but *ruach* is eternal.

If this were not so, we would not be here today. If *hebel* had the final word, then after the crucifixion, the disciples would have said, "Everything passes. Our Lord is gone. It is all vanity and chasing after the wind."

"All the way to heaven is heaven." The eternal is found in time.

My father was a successful businessman. He was the vice president of a firm that manufactured sweaters. In 1972, the company went through a massive restructuring and he lost his job. At 53, he confronted the noonday devil.

The next years were very difficult for him because his faith in the ethics of business was shattered. He had sacrificed so much—time with his family or hobbies or friends—for his job. And he discovered it was all *hebel, vanity, a chasing after wind*. But the good news is that in the remaining years of his working life, he found more *ruach* than before.

My father and mother bought a farm and moved there. They started their own business. They had animals: chickens, a horse, goats, pigs, dogs, birds. They had more time for friends and more time for their kids.

So maybe the point is this. When we feel gripped by *hebel*, when we confront the noonday devil, we will feel as if we have no time. But if we will breathe deeply, if we will take in God's *ruach*, or the resurrecting wind, then we will discover that in every moment there is all the time and the grace that we need.

Promises That Last

ZEPHANIAH 1:7, 12–18; PSALM 90 OR 90:1–8, 12; I THESSALONIANS 5:1–10; MATTHEW 25:14–15, 19–29

For God has destined us not for wrath but for obtaining salvation through our Lord Jesus Christ, who died for us, so that whether we are awake or asleep we may live with him.
I THESSALONIANS 5:9–10

We have a copy of Paul's letters to the Thessalonians, but have you ever wondered about Paul's mail? Did the postman pass by his box every single day? Was Paul singing "Please Mr. Postman" with the Sherrells because no one writes him back?

I was in Sewanee, Tennessee, three weeks ago and had time to use the University of the South library. As I was poking around in the stacks, I came across an old box with some letters in it. Way down on the bottom, I found an old frayed, yellow document. When I opened it, I could not believe my eyes. Here was a letter from the Thessalonians to Paul.

That's right! A two-thousand-year-old letter. I am translating his working from the Greek—and taking some license:

November 14, A.D. 49

To Paul—Apostle of Our Lord, Jesus Christ

Greetings and Peace,

Thank you for your visit. You left in sort of a huff so we didn't get to thank you in person. Sorry that some of our Jewish friends got so upset during your talk.

We never thought they'd riot like that. Don't worry, we'll cover the damage costs. I don't really know what to say. It was a tough audience. The food thing didn't go over too well. It's probably okay to talk about the Gentiles eating whatever they want, but maybe next time you shouldn't order barbecue just to make them happy. It isn't worth it.

Anyway, we heard that you told Timothy that you were really down when you left. As a matter of fact, the rumor is that you said if the

Thessalonians became Christians you'd eat your *yarmulke*. Well, *mazel tov*, Paul—do you want that *yarmulke* with lox or plain?

That's right—the whole crowd signed on the dotted line. We now have a full house every Sunday night—but . . . but we do have a few questions:

Most folks have quieted down over the food thing, and we are even okay with the circumcision thing—especially the Gentiles. But . . . what about this end of the world? You put the fear of God into these folks.

We've got people over here storing up water and food. One whole family has quit their jobs and sit in their lawn chairs staring at the sky, looking for Jesus to float down. And people are backing up their computers like crazy. Everyone has canceled their airline tickets for Rome. No one is paying their taxes, since the computers will be down. So what is the deal? Are you telling us we converted just in time to get leveled?

I have to say that some folks feel like you didn't read them the fine print when they signed on. We thought the whole deal was love, and then we just turn around to find all this doom and gloom stuff. After all, what's the point of becoming Christian if it's all over? And if it is all over, what will happen to us? Are people lifted up in order of their conversion? Are you sure our names are on the list?

So here's the thing: now that we know about this end of the world stuff, what should we do? Should we go to our fallout shelters and hunker down! Are we in the clear or not?

Write when you can, Paulie. There's folks that think you are kind of a shyster.

All the best—

Thess alone without you.

No wonder Paul wrote them right back. He probably knew the people would react this way. It's human nature. Something new comes along and it seems like it's just the thing. At first everything is wonderful. Then after some time you start looking closer at what you've gotten into, and you see all these little details you never saw before. Suddenly you start to think: This isn't what I thought it would be at all. So two weeks after the marriage you find out that your spouse squeezes the toothpaste from the middle of the tube, or she introduces you to all those weird relatives you've never heard of before.

When I joined my college fraternity, I thought I was in the "in" crowd. I thought I had arrived. A month later one of the brothers got locked out of his room by his roommate. Slightly irritated, he went down the hall, borrowed someone's shotgun and blew the door down. At that point, the "out" crowd didn't look so bad to me.

We always have second thoughts because the more we live with any new thing, the more complex it becomes. We always suspect that there is some odious surprise in the small print.

But the truth is—we always stumble over complexity and change. We'd like the world to be simple and static, but it never is. There is always more to any experience than we can perceive. And just when we finally do grasp some of the complexity of the situation, everything changes and we have to start all over.

When something first happens—we join a group; we fall in love; we get a new job—we love that initial glow. Everything is pure elation. We want to stay in the honeymoon forever, where everything is simple and static. But soon our eyes get open and the full moon fades, and the honey jar gets empty and after a while we begin to see all sorts of curiosities we never saw before.

Remember in your high school annuals when your friends would write: "Promise you'll never change"?

We'd like to make that promise—we'd like for the good parts of our life to never change. But they will and they do. The question is not whether or not we will change; we will. The question is how can we hold onto the essential truth that lasts? As Jesus told Peter: How can we become the "rock" so that there is a core of constancy amid complexity and change?

So Paul tells the Thessalonians what all of us need to hear and can accept: We are changing. We live in time, and because we live in time, this experience, this age, this life will end. It's like a woman being pregnant; she cannot stay that way forever. Because this world will end (remember, Jesus has promised that it will end), we assume that everything ends with it. We assume that when what we know is gone, life stops. So we want to protect ourselves from the great transition. But we have our task all upside down. We are to hold onto what lasts. What lasts is faith and love and hope. Just as in a marriage, the only thing that finally lasts is love. Everything else is change.

Today's scripture translation calls for us to "put on the breastplate of faith," but a more accurate translation is: "Since we have put on [past tense] the breastplate of faith." The good news is that God has already prepared us for complexity and change. God has put on us the divine armor. All we must do is wear it—use it to move forward. Instead of fear, God has adorned us with faith. Instead of estrangement, God has covered us with love. And instead of despair or cynicism, God has anointed us with hope.

For the truth is simple. Once you are God's—once Jesus Christ lays hands on you—you are his. That is the plan; that is the only plan. As Paul says, God has destined us not for wrath, but for obtaining salvation through our Lord Jesus Christ. Salvation—wholeness in Christ—is our destiny. That's the rock. That's what is constant and simple and true. Once we know that, then we can be open to complexity and change. Let the end come and go. Let all the surprises of the small print come and go.

Who cares? Rapture—Y2K—millennium—hair loss—new prayer book—new building—new bishop—illness—death—who cares? As Paul says elsewhere: *Jesus Christ is the same yesterday and today and forever* (Hebrews 13:8).

What matters is not how things change or how complex our lives become. What matters is the core truth that Jesus Christ is in this with us, holding on to us and bringing us to him. The whole point of the second coming is not the destruction of the world or the meltdown of our computers; the whole point is that we will be with Christ and he will be with us.

How can we hold onto the essential truth that lasts?

I thought of a story about transition—about learning to see in a time of change. It's called "Tell Me a Riddle" by Tillie Olsen. It's about a Jewish couple. The woman is dying, and her husband feels as if he is trapped by the small print. He didn't bargain for this when he signed on. He wants to know if everything is over in this transition. Just as the Thessalonians want to know about the second coming.

As his wife is dying, his granddaughter comes to him and tells him to remember who his wife really is—to remember what lasts. She says to him:

Grandaddy, Grandaddy, don't cry. She is not there. She promised me. On the last day, she said she would go back to when she first heard music, a little girl on the road of the village where she was born. She promised me. It is a wedding day and they dance, while the flutes so joyous and vibrant tremble in the air. . . . Grandaddy, it is all right, she promised me.

The Thessalonians have been promised, too, and so have we. And this is the promise: Neither death, nor the end-time, nor any small print will separate us from the love of Jesus Christ.

The Melody of the Future

 Acts 13:15–16, 26–33 (34–39) or Numbers
27:12–23; Psalm 100; Revelation 7:9–17;
John 10:22–30

*They will hunger no more, and thirst no more . . . for the
Lamb at the center of the throne will be their shepherd, and he
will guide them to springs of the water of life, and God will
wipe away every tear from their eyes.*
Revelation 7:16–17

The problem with being a younger brother is that you can never catch
up. You can grow taller, you can become stronger, and maybe even
smarter. But your older brother is always going to be ahead of you.

When I was around five or so, I found this very frustrating. My
brother Dick was seven, and I couldn't figure out how to overcome the
gap. Finally, someone told me, *"One day, one day, you'll be as old as your
brother. Then you'll do all the things he does now."* And I thought of myself
differently. I wasn't just a five-year-old. I was a future seven-year-old.
One day I was going to go to Grace Elementary School and summer
camp and play Little League. It was as if I had double vision. I saw
myself as I was and as I would be.

The two visions inform one another. Our sense of our future
shapes our sense of ourselves in this moment. And our present situation gives a context for our dreams of what will be. A five-year-old has
five-year-old dreams. My dreams only extended to becoming a pro foot-
ball player or a rock star. I didn't know about literature or colleges, or
so many other things.

The point is we live in time, real time, the weaving-together of past,
present, and future. The present is never an isolated moment. We come
from somewhere and we are going somewhere else.

The past gives a foundation for this moment, and the future gives
a purpose to this moment.

Jean Houston, the writer of *The Mythic Life*, says: *"If you do not
mythologize, you will pathologize."* That is, you must see your story in the

light of a larger story to have a meaningful life. You must have some mythic context or your life doesn't make sense. Myth gives us a past, a pattern for the present, and a future.

Which brings us to that strange book—the book of Revelation. Instead of wondering about the seals and the great tribulation and all the blood, let's do some history.

We believe the book of Revelation was written around A.D. 100. The author, John of Patmos, addresses the seven churches that were facing persecution in what we now call Turkey. The Romans were demanding that these churches acknowledge the emperor as a god. Refusal to do so was certain death. John of Patmos writes a very strange book. He gives no advice for their present dilemma. He doesn't talk about conflict management. He doesn't tell them how to handle the Romans. Instead, he gives them a vision of the future.

He holds out the promises of what will be: The ones who come through the great ordeal *"will hunger no more, and thirst no more; the sun will not strike them, nor any scorching heat; for the Lamb . . . will be their shepherd, and he will guide them to springs of the water of life, and God will wipe away every tear from their eyes."* John of Patmos wants the churches to hope.

Someone said, *"Hope is hearing the melody of the future."* As we hear that melody, we have that double vision that my five-year-old self had: *I am part of the present, but I am also part of what will be.*

Now it makes sense why people living next to the desert see their future in these terms: No more thirst . . . no more scorching heat . . . and being led to the springs of the water of life. Perhaps in our middle-class, industrial world we can't relate to these things. We have too many water fountains and too much air-conditioning to grasp these images. We could easily write our own vision: No more random violence . . . no more estrangement from one another . . . no more racism or sexism . . . no more hatred or degradation, and so forth.

But instead of rewriting Revelation, let's hold onto what we can. The last image is not limited to desert people: *"God will wipe away every tear from their eyes."*

Tears are a universal language, and they come in every age of life: The tears of childhood—broken toys and lost soccer games and friends who say hurtful things. And then there's adolescence, with all its dreams and disappointments—being jilted by girlfriends and boyfriends, and your body that refuses to behave and look right. The tears of middle-age—parents who die, children you cannot protect, jobs that don't feed the soul, spouses who become strangers. And then our last tears for all that wasn't—for all you cannot control or make better. And that's just our private lives. There's also war and poverty and famine and random violence. The tears of Vietnam, Bosnia, Rwanda, Oklahoma City, the Twin Towers, Iraq.

If we only have the present, then our tears just wash down our faces and into the ground. Without a future, without a mythic story, all we can do is protect ourselves from a scary world that demands our tears. All we can do is ignore the world around us that makes us weep. This world only makes sense if we know that God is on our side and leading us to a time when *"God will wipe away every tear from our eyes."*

It's why the civil rights workers always sang. "We shall overcome." It's why Terry Anderson repeated the Twenty-third Psalm while in captivity.

We are not people trapped in digital time. We are part of history. We stand on the shoulders of those who came before us, and we look to the day when *God's kingdom comes on earth as in heaven.*

Amid all our tears in this world, we look for a tearless world. We don't see ourselves as just five years old or seven years old, or even forty-seven years old. We also see ourselves as part of a history that leads to God's kingdom. We have that double vision—seeing the present tears, yet also seeing that a tearless future changes everything. It means we are empowered to wipe the tears of all those who weep. It means we have courage to work to change all that causes people to suffer. For we know the promise, and, therefore, we work to make it real.

In Mark Helprin's novel, *A Soldier of the Great War*, he writes of a priest who comforts a young soldier who is dying:

> He had gathered the boy in his arms, and he was bathed in his blood, But he held him the way you would hold a baby, and he cried, and he talked to him until he died.
> "I can't see," the boy said. . . . That was the only time Father Michele quoted the Bible to him.
> He said, "Like a swallow mine eyes fail with looking upward."

The soldier was dying quickly. His soul was halfway to another place.

The priest said, "Where you are going there is no fear and there is no dying.

"Your mother and father will be there. They'll hold you like a baby. They'll stroke your head, and you'll sleep in their arms, in bliss."

"I wish it would be so," the boy said.

"It will be so," Father Michele answered, and he repeated it again and again, "It will be so, it will be so," until the boy died.[12]

Wherever we are—when the tears of the present run down our faces—let us remember the promises God has made, and say to ourselves, and say to our broken world—*"It will be so."*

---

12. Mark Helprin, *A Soldier of the Great War* (New York: Harcourt Brace Jovanovich, 1991), 770.

Won by Grace

 AMOS 6:1–7; PSALM 146 OR 146:4–9; I TIMOTHY
6:11–19; LUKE 16:19–31

*Fight the good fight of the faith; take hold of the eternal life, to
which you were called.*
I TIMOTHY 6:12

At long last I have finally discovered my true calling: I am the coach for
my daughter Marie's under-eight soccer team, the Blue Streak.

Last Saturday we had our first game. Now we weren't going into
this cold. We *had* practiced, and most of the girls have played before.
But still, it was the first time they had played as a team. When the game
started, I admit we were a little hesitant. It was like trying to find someone's house in a strange city. You've got a map and directions, but reality is a lot more complicated than those red and black lines. So the Blue
Streak didn't exactly *streak* for the first few minutes. Instead, the girls
sort of wandered around the field. They looked like Japanese tourists in
New York City.

And then an amazing thing happened. Suddenly they got it. They
grabbed hold of the game of soccer and began to play. It was as if they
just woke up and opened their eyes. Something inside clicked and they
played.

Some of us never open our eyes and never grab hold of life. At the
beginning of *Walden*, Henry David Thoreau writes, "I went to the
woods because . . . I did not wish to live what was *not life*, living is so
dear." So much of our society lives a *not life*, a half life, or a life where
the object becomes to get through the day. And so we are on automatic.

I drive from Nashville to Franklin everyday. When I get in my car
in the morning, I turn on some automatic pilot, and I remember very
little of what I see until I get to St. Paul's. It's what we call "dead time."
And so we try to fill it in to make it bearable. Music, television, or buying things that no one needs. Or we turn to compulsive behavior: alcohol, food, sex. These are efforts to survive "dead time." In the hope of
feeling alive, we put some buffer between us and life itself. The reason

109

Jesus criticizes the rich so strongly is because they are again able to buy so many buffers. They have the power to insulate themselves from life.

In the parable today, even in hades the rich man still treats Lazarus like a slave. He wants to snap his fingers and order some bottled water. He wants to push away the pain. That's the danger of wealth. Money enables us to remove ourselves from real life, the life of death and resurrection, the life of pain and joy. Money gives the illusion that we are self-sufficient and protected and in control. But St. Paul has a very a different thing to say; he encourages us to *"take hold of the eternal life . . . take hold of the life that really is life."*

Heaven is not just a place that Lazarus and the righteous go after death. Nor is hell just a place that the proud and sinful are sent as punishment. Whoever takes hold of eternal life lives in heaven *right now.* Whoever refuses eternal life lives in hell on earth.

What is heaven? Heaven is life that really is life. And hell? Hell is death.

Through Jesus Christ, God offers eternal life. God invites people to take hold of that life. It's the life that is whole; the life that contains all the opposites: life and death; pain and joy; separateness and community. It's the life of resurrection that lies beyond the tomb. Jesus Christ saves us from death because he shows us the way to resurrected life.

And resurrection is not about fear. It's not about protecting yourself; nor is it about filling your life with diversions. It's about being free to witness the grace that is all about us.

It may look like there are 5,000 people and no food, but if we look again, it's a feast.

It may look like there is no wine at the wedding, but if we look again, the water is transformed into wine.

Jesus calls us to stop being afraid that life isn't going to be what we want it to be and taste life as it is, in all its sweetness and its bitterness. For despite what our money tells us, there is no buffer from suffering. You cannot buy enough things or find enough diversions to make it go away. There is only the not-life of hell or the life—the real life—of heaven. That real life is the life of faith. That is the life that knows that every moment God holds out the bread of heaven for us to eat, but we have to let go of our fears and our need to control and take hold.

When the Blue Streak woke up that day, the ball rolled in front of one of our players, and suddenly she was a blur. She ran down the field, dodged two opponents, and kicked the ball into the goal. It was if her enthusiasm were contagious. The other girls took hold. Oh, by the way, her name really is *Grace*.

The Blue Streak did win that first game, but they are not going to win every game. But despite what Vince Lombardi said, that's not the point. The point is to be alive—to wake up—to take hold of the life that really is life. When that happens, we will know that heaven, the kingdom of God, is among us.

The Other World

 Acts 9:1–19a or Jeremiah 32:36–41;
Revelation 5:6–14; John 21:1–14

Jesus said to them, "Come and have breakfast."
John 21:12

How far we have come.

We began with those important disembodied pronouncements: In the beginning was the Word. It sounded as if God were speaking through the heavens in the voice of Orson Welles. And then we got the signs: Changing water into wine. Healing the sick with a word. Feeding the 5,000. Even raising the dead.

I feel as if we've been in a benevolent version of *Raiders of the Lost Ark*. Instead of someone dying every thirty seconds, someone is being made whole. And I am hooked. The action is fast-paced, and the special effects are amazing all the time.

As we draw near the close, I know the ending is going to be a blockbuster. In the first resurrection account, Jesus comes through locked doors; not bad. In the second account, Thomas gets to poke around in Jesus' wounds. So far, so good. We are set for something spectacular, even bigger than when they open the ark at the end of *Raiders*.

And the story begins okay. The disciples do catch 153 fish with one toss. That's not quite as good as walking through walls, but look what he did with two fish earlier. By my calculations, with this number Jesus ought to be able to feed around 380,000 people. But suddenly Spielberg isn't directing anymore. All the special effects get turned off. Jesus turns to the disciples and says, *"Come and have breakfast."* For a moment we feel as if we're in a different movie.

But the longer I sit with this story, the more sense it makes. This is the same movie. In fact, this breakfast scene is the only logical conclusion to the script. Because this gospel is about how we grow into relationships.

Our pattern of human relationships is like that of Christ with us. In the initial stage we are nervous. This is a new person, totally

112

unfamiliar. We are dazzled by this new world. Everything seems miraculous and larger than life. In this honeymoon stage, everything is perfect. It's as if our black-and-white world has been flipped to color.

Remember your high school infatuations? In the tenth grade I fell in love with Karen Bell. I wrote her name all over my notebook; I sent her presents; I thought about her all the time. My crush on her kept me at an emotional peak for two months. But gradually I wore out, the honeymoon always ends, and we go from magical time to ordinary time. In the tenth grade I didn't want to change to ordinary time, so I went from Karen Bell to Alice Fisher. I got a new notebook and started all over again.

So often we look at Jesus the way I looked at Karen Bell. We want to feel as if something amazing is taking place—as if Jesus is in charge of our spiritual entertainment system. And he is supposed to keep us stimulated—as if he were running a cosmic TV show. We want to stay in the honeymoon phase forever.

Alan Jones asks, *"Do I worship God or do I worship my experience of God?"* If I worship my experience of God, then I am waiting for a spiritual high: God is the provider and I am the consumer.

This relationship keeps Jesus distant from us. Jesus is a miracle worker; He is our protector; our shepherd. But we keep him at arm's length because we are afraid if we become too intimate, our idealized picture of this relationship will vanish.

I was not really in love with Karen Bell. I was in love with my ideas of Karen Bell. And rather than give those up to be with a real person, I went and found Alice Fisher.

We hold onto our idealized picture of Jesus because we like to watch him change the world, instead of risking being changed ourselves. For in intimate relationships, anything can happen.

I am not discounting Jesus' ability to do miracles, nor am I denigrating Christ's presence in people's lives in startling ways. But I am saying that Jesus is calling us into a deeper, more mature relationship. That call means we must let go of our formulas and our fantasies and fall in love with Christ.

Have you noticed how quiet, how simple, genuine love is? People who are really in love find doing the simple tasks with one another miraculous. The ordinary tasks become sacramental. Patrick White says,

"There is another world, but it's the same as this one." The goal is not to get out of this life. The goal is to embrace our lives as they are and to discover in the fiber of the world itself the grace we need.

It's like the ending of the film, *The Fisher King.* The characters discover that the Holy Grail is not some silver chalice in some cave in Palestine. The Holy Grail is a Little League cup. *"There is another world, but it's the same as this one."*

Jesus has come to bring us into this other world that is the same as this one.

So we have come a long way. It may be that all the signs of Jesus are pointing beyond the miraculous to something more amazing. For Jesus did not come to give a miracle show. The Word was made flesh for a simple, ordinary reason: to be with us and to show us what love is.

The point of love is to love—not to astonish, not to convince, not to "wow" us. After all the miraculous signs, Jesus gives a very simple invitation: *"Come and have breakfast."*

The huge catch is forgotten; the unbroken net is not mentioned. For a while no one talks. Just a silent call to let go of our fantasy of the superstar and to let the real Jesus into the ordinary rhythms of our daily lives.

Called by God

PSALM 71:1–17; JEREMIAH 1:4–10; 1 CORINTHIANS
15:1–11; LUKE 4:14–21

*"Before I formed you in the womb I knew you, and before you
were born I consecrated you; I appointed you a prophet to the
nations."*
JEREMIAH 1:5

The day it happened was a homecoming because the words came into
his heart from somewhere outside yet it seemed absolutely familiar.

It was as if he heard his own voice for the first time. He touched
his mouth to see if he had spoken. In that moment, he could see. The
confusion that so often clouded his world lifted.

So often he had wondered: *Will we get the Assyrians off our back for
good? Can we trust the Babylonians? Are we going to be free? Does God want us
to go to the Temple day after day to worship or is there another way?*

He wondered about these things. In fact, he thought more about
these things than he did about getting on with his life. Everyone said it
was time to think about following in his father's footsteps—marriage—
a home—a life. But he thought about Judah and faithfulness and
oppression.

So when the voice came inside him, at first he didn't know what it was:
"Jeremiah—Go and deliver."

He looked around, hoping there was another Jeremiah. *Who me? I'm
fourteen years old. I'm a freshman in high school. I don't even have a license. Go
where? Deliver whom?*

Even as he said it, he knew. He had always known somewhere in his
heart that he was meant for this kind of service. He was just scared and
he didn't want to look foolish.

Every time he had heard some little voice saying his name— he had
brushed it off. He told himself *it's just my imagination—maybe it's something I ate.* But this time, it was too loud. This time—he felt someone
touch his mouth and it burned. That touch ran all the way through him.
And Jeremiah knew that he wasn't alone. He knew that God was with

him, and although he did not know where he was going, he was ready
to go.

It's a nice story, isn't it? And it must be true because it's in the Bible,
but what about us? Are we called? Or is that just for the Bible folks? If
we are, what does it mean? What happens when you are called?

Well—the first thing is you never feel adequate. It's an automatic
reaction. Jeremiah says, *"I am only a boy."* Moses says, *"I can't talk very well."*
Isaiah says, *"I am not holy enough."* When God calls us, our first response
is always *"Not me. You got the wrong person. Whatever you need, I don't have it."*

Up to a point—and the point is where we give in and say, *"Okay I'll
go anyway"*—up to a point our reservations are actually healthy because
they force us to focus on what God is doing and not on what we are
capable of doing. That's why the answers to the questions in our baptism are "I will, with God's help." That is, I will so long as God does
the real work.

Jeremiah looked at Judah who had been captive to the Assyrians
forever, and he could not image how he—only a boy—could do much
about his country's plight. Moses looked at the Israelites captive to
Egypt—and he could not imagine how he could do much. But in a
strange sort of way, the sign of being called is this sense of inadequacy.

If someone comes up to you and says *"God has called me to save
Athens—and I am completely prepared to do it,"* then run.

In the *Lord of the Rings,* those people who think they are the best
person to carry the ring are exactly the ones you don't want anywhere
near so much power. Instead, the one who is chosen is the small hobbit
who only says, *"I will take the ring, though I do not know the way."*

The point is our own sense of inadequacy points us to God's ade-
quacy. Of course, Jeremiah doesn't know how to bring Judah back into
righteousness. But God isn't asking him to know—God is asking him
to participate in what God is doing. Jeremiah goes not because he
knows what to say—but because God assures him that God will put the
words into his mouth.

So, yes we are hesitant; yes, we do resist, but we go because in going we
become more of who we are. God tells Jeremiah this isn't a new thing:

> *Before you were born, I consecrated you; I appointed you a prophet
> to the nations.*

Our calling is not so much about what we do—it's about who we are. One day we hear a voice deep within and we remember what we were born for—that voice within us beckons us to step out. At first we don't know what the voice is—but if we listen, it's our voice saying our name. If we listen, our voice has the echo of God's voice—and we know if we do not follow, we will never be completely alive.

Somewhere in his soul, Jeremiah has always known he is a prophet. Because there is no market for prophets, he hasn't listened to that voice. Of course, in his heart, he knows his deafness makes him a little less alive. Every time he looks at the Assyrians, he knows in his heart, he should speak out. Every time he looks at his fellow Israelites, part of him dies as he stays silent.

Each of us is called to follow that voice within—that beckons us to manifest as who we are. That voice is actually our meeting place with God. There is a great joy in following God's calling because for the first time in our lives, we fit. If you are a painter and you have embraced your calling, you'd paint for free. (As a matter of fact, you probably do paint for free.) It's who you are.

As the poet William Stafford writes:

> *Some time when the river is ice ask me*
> *mistakes I have made. Ask me whether*
> *What I have done is my life.*

He means the greatest mistake is to live what is not our life.

Jeremiah feels inadequate—then he embraces that voice as his own.

Finally he is called to go out on behalf of God. Isn't it amazing that no one in the Bible is called to go shopping or go to Super Bowl parties? God doesn't call us to serve ourselves. We are called to play our part in what God is doing. We are called to serve in the transformation of the world. Jeremiah is given power to pluck up and to pull down— to build and to plant, because it's God's plan to pluck up, pull down— to build and to plant.

When our inner calling is true, it is always matched by service to the world—Frederick Buechner's wonderful definition of vocation: *"The place God calls you to is the place where your deep gladness and the world's deep hunger meet."* And it is always hard.

The world is not real excited about being plucked up or pulled down.

Many people did not want to hear Jeremiah or Amos or Jesus or St. Francis or Dorothy Day or Martin Luther King, Jr. Many people were not excited about the call of Picasso or William Faulkner or Frank Lloyd Wright. Many people will not be excited about your call either. They'll say to you—you're just a girl; you're not ready; it won't work.

But when that happens remember the best part of the call. Every time you step out to follow that inner voice, God whispers in your ear "I am with you and I am with you and I am with you."

The Deepest Longing

Sermons for Transitions

Will You Say "Yes"?
An Ordination Sermon

 Isaiah 6:1–8; Ephesians 4:7, 11–16; John 6:35–38

I was eighteen years old. Like many eighteen-year-olds I was idealistic and hopeful. Remember what the 1960s were like? Filled with dreams and visions. The Age of Aquarius, as we used to sing. Eighteen-year-olds thought about ending the war in Vietnam. We thought about ending racism and poverty. We felt that we were on the verge of a new era.

Now, I come from a family of Democrats. We are what's called in the South "Yellow Dog Democrats." At 18, I knew there was only one person who could lead this country into the promised land. That was Bobby Kennedy; he was the hope of the future. I was a Bobby Kennedy groupie. I read his speeches. I wore his buttons.

Well, one June evening I stayed up much too late at a party. The next morning my radio alarm went off and in a half-awake state I heard the news—Bobby Kennedy had been shot in California. I felt the breath whoosh out of my body. There was no future—only blankness. It was as if the world had conspired to say *No. No* to everything I hoped for and dreamed of. I did not know then what I know now: whenever the world says *No*—that is the time God asks us to say *Yes*.

The year that King Uzziah died is the same year Bobby Kennedy died. It's the year the world says *No* to all we had dreamed. It's the year Isaiah woke to find all the breath whooshed out of him. And with good reason: King Uzziah had brought Judah prosperity and security. He extended the territory, he developed trade and agriculture. But then he contracted leprosy and died. Isaiah knew that dark times were ahead. He knew that the Assyrians who had been howling on the borders would descend upon Judah.

In the year King Uzziah died, the world said *No* to all of Isaiah's would-be dreams and hopes. And yet—and yet—in that time God asked Isaiah to say *Yes*. God said to Isaiah—"I know the world is in a mess. I know that you are not being sent to proclaim the word that the world wants to hear, but I am asking you to say the word the world needs to hear.

"So will you say 'yes' in a time when the world says 'no'? Will you say 'yes' in a time when the world is filled with fear—when people withdraw into themselves and forget how to cope and stop thinking about the common good?"

Hannah, I haven't forgotten you. This really is a sermon about your ordination. I know it's not new to you that we live in confusing times. Your work in hospitals tells you that day after day. And your journey has been a journey through the wilderness.

Many times the church, your society, and even people close to you have been the voices that have said *No*. Many times you have come to a wall, and it's felt as if King Uzziah or Bobby Kennedy, or maybe even part of Hannah has died. But you are here because God has spoken to you through the voices of friends and teachers and people who love you. And every time it's felt as if the world has said *No*, through these voices God has asked you to say *Yes*.

You are here today to be ordained a priest in Christ's church, and after today you will be different. Yes, you'll still be Hannah, and that creative, bold spirit will still reside in your soul. You'll still be the only person in the history of the School of Theology at Sewanee who gave a sermon sitting at a potter's wheel throwing a pot. And the only person who for her final project in Scripture class turned in a painting with tennis shoes stuck on the canvas.

But after today people will look at you differently. You'll be what Henri Nouwen calls a "living reminder"; a reminder that God has never promised us a life without suffering. Jesus never said that we would be understood or appreciated. Nowhere did God say that the world would say "yes."

But God promises something much greater, as we heard in Philippians today. God promises the peace of God, which surpasses all understanding. And that is what we say "yes" to. You are to remind people of that peace. Hannah, you are to be an icon, a window.

Through you and your ministry, people are to see into the mystery—
the one mystery—that Christ is always dying, that Christ is always
being risen, and that Christ is always coming again.

Our peace comes from knowing that is the pattern of the world.
That mystery is the "yes" we are to proclaim, no matter how loudly the
world says "no": Even if King Uzziah and Bobby Kennedy die every
day, we know that if we will walk through that brokenness, we will find
the land of resurrection beyond. For the light is always stronger than
the dark. Life is always stronger than death. Once we know that then we
are free to say "yes."

Hannah, I give voice to the joy that all these people here feel today.
Not just because we love you, and we do. But because in your heart and
soul and life you remind us that the mission of the church is not litur-
gical correctness or ethical purity. The Church was not formed to set
the rules of the world, or to put on an esthetically splendid show.

The mission of the Church is the transformation of a broken
world into the kingdom of God. Our calling as Christians is to be
transformed into the likeness of Christ, and we can only do that by saying "yes" to God's love and by allowing that "yes" to reverberate in our
lives and in our world. For finally our faith is not in a set of rules. Nor
is it in our abilities to figure out the world's problems. Our faith is in
Jesus Christ. Our faith is that the risen Christ is loving a broken world
into wholeness, and that's what we are called to say *yes* to.

Hannah, I don't think your "Exodus phase" is over. I don't think it
ever will be. I think you'll still wander in the wilderness. I think that's
where anyone who is real lives. But as a priest you will teach those pil-
grims you encounter how to hold hands, and how to love one another,
and how to feed one another. And your little band will discover the
oasis of grace from time to time, until slowly all of you know in your
bones that Jesus Christ travels with you.

And your feet are his feet.

And your hands are his hands.

And one day one of your people will say, "Hannah, thanks for
teaching us to say *yes* when the world said *no.*

Hannah, you are here today to say "yes" to God's will, even though
so often it feels as if King Uzziah has just died and the whole world
is saying *no.* Take heart, for although you do not know how this will

work out, you do not know what shape your ministry will take, you do know this: The way is dying and rising with Christ. You are called to be Hannah and show your people what growing into the likeness of Christ looks like.

As you feel the hands of your bishop and these priests on your head and shoulders, know that they are also the hands of all the friends, people who have led you to this place—not just the ones you have known physically, but that great cloud of witnesses. Because when one soul says *yes* to the call of God, that *yes* reverberates.

We hear the echoes of men like Isaiah. And we hear the echoes of women like Mary Magdalene. And then we know, know in our hearts, that the foundation of the world is God's *Yes* to us.

The Deepest Longing
A Burial Sermon

ISAIAH 25:6–9; ROMANS 8:14–19, 34–35, 37–39;
JOHN 14:1–6

We are here to remember.

To "re-member" is to reconnect to another. It is once again to join as members of something larger than ourselves. So today we are first here to remember the life of Richard Taylor, to hold up his life as a witness.

Second, we are here to remember our grief at his passing; to be joined together in the community of tears; to let those waters come from deep inside us and join us together.

And third, we are here to be remembered to God and God's Son Jesus Christ, and through my father to the great cloud of witnesses that are the body of Christ.

To remember, to remember the past, to remember our grief, to remember God.

First, to remember the past.

We remember Dick Taylor in different ways: father, husband, friend, neighbor, churchman. I can't capture everything he was. I can only remember him as my father.

My father had a large heart. He felt things strongly. He was often wildly happy and sometimes very angry. But he was not a neutral person. He also knew how to have a good time. He loved to eat too much and drink too much and just do too much. He used to call parties "rallies": and I always imagined that he was trying to cheer the world on. He was trying to rally people to forget the stupidity of our world for a little while and step into some joyful circle.

And if this is really Dick Taylor's funeral, then we should laugh and cry. And after the service some of you ought to go to your cars and find a bottle and stand around and have a drink. He would have wanted it that way.

When I remember my father, most of all I think of him as an idealist—he wanted more from life than life could give him. A devout Democrat, he despaired when Richard Nixon beat Hubert Humphrey, and that frustration only increased as he lived through eight long years of Ronald Reagan.

Often, I thought my father just didn't live at the right time, because he was one of the few gentlemen I knew, and he expected the world to be a place of manners, thoughtfulness, and fairness. Although he was often disappointed, he never abandoned that code of behavior. He was a gentleman.

I remember that all my life when I would ask my father what to do, he never told me directly. But he would in turn ask me, *"What's important? What's important?"* He thought that if you lived your life by moral principles, things would turn out okay.

But maybe he did live in the wrong time because our world is often not a place of manners and thoughtfulness and fairness. Sometimes our world is a place of bombings and MTV and people sleeping in the street. So I remember my father as an idealist, a man who wanted more than this broken world could give. I remember Dick Taylor as a man of passion and courage and faith.

As each of us remembers him, we are remembered to one another in our common grief. C. S. Lewis said that the pain of losing someone is that we miss those parts of ourselves that only that person could bring out and that's why we grieve Dick Taylor. He was a person who could make you laugh and make you think and make you angry. But he always made you feel something. We will miss my father's capacity to make simple things seem important, more fun, more alive.

Even at the end, he made us laugh. Last week I walked into his room in ICU with a red shirt on, and he wrote a note saying: "Porter, I didn't know it's Pentecost."

As I drove here yesterday, I thought of how often my father would go on the beach when we were children and sit in the sun all day until he was what he called "a bronze God"; which was really red as a lobster. I didn't know those days on the beach were Pentecost, either. But they were. So many days with him were. And we will miss them.

As we feel the loss of those parts that only he could bring forth, we are remembered to one another in our loss.

But we are also here to be remembered to God, and to celebrate God's remembering of Richard Taylor to God's self. For when I think of all my father's longings and disappointments:

His longing to work in places that respected quality.

His longing for a world that was fair.

His longing for health.

And his longing for a family that had become spread all over the country to come home.

I see him now in the only place that he could ever find true peace. As the Lord God wipes away the tears from my father's face, his blind eyes will again come to life and he will see and he will be remembered.

I imagine him speaking with Christ. Christ asks him, "Dick, what do you want?"

And like a child, my father is at first afraid to ask. So he starts small: "Will there be booze in heaven? . . . And rallies?"

"Yes, if you want," Christ answers.

"Will there be Republicans?"

"Yes, but don't worry. They have been changed just like you, into likeness of Me."

And then my father gains speed.

"What about Justice? Good, clean work? No more pain? No more disappointments?"

"Will I see?"

"Yes, Dick, all of that."

"Will my family be here? Will we all be home at last?"

"Yes. Yes. Yes."

And Christ holds him close as a father holds his child and whispers into his ear: *"Yes. Yes. Yes!"*

"And Dick, you'll be with me and I'll be with you, *forever.*"

Rocking with the Saints

A Burial Sermon

ISAIAH 25:6–9; ROMANS 8:14–19, 34–35, 37–39; JOHN 14:1–6

We are here to do three things: to celebrate the life of Ransom Spann Richardson, to grieve our loss, and to give thanks to God.

First, to celebrate his life.

I had the privilege of knowing Ran for forty-six years, and the longer I knew him, the more I respected him. In many ways, Ran didn't fit our time: in an age of speed, of things going faster and faster, Ran Richardson was the slowest man alive.

He operated on a different time zone: "Ran Time." My father, Dick Taylor, humorously used to call him "Speedy Gonzales." but Ran knew where he wanted to go. And he knew he would get there at his own pace.

In a fast world, he was slow, and in a *me-first*world, he was kind. Has there ever been a nicer person than Ran Richardson? As a priest, I try to do a few good works, but, I confess, I want credit for them. But Ran did things for people because he thought you ought to help people out.

Jesus told us to be leaven for the world. Leaven is slow and quiet; but it is what gives us our daily bread. And Ran's kindness was that kind of leaven. I know whenever my family needed him, he was there. And the day before he died, Ran was mowing a neighbor's lawn. We think of a philanthropist as someone who gives money for charitable causes, but Ran Richardson was a philanthropist in the deepest sense.

Finally, in an age that believes you can invent yourself, Ran knew that the past counts. I think he had a map in his head—a map of Fluds and Richardsons, and Mannings, and Moores and Gibbs and Hamptons. Whenever he met someone you could hear the wheels turn as he placed them in relation. But he taught us that *where you come from is part of who you are.*

In a world of Dennis Rodman and Madonna, Ransom Richardson may seem out of step, but for those of us who knew him and loved him, his life gave grace and meaning to our world. So we are here to celebrate his life and to give thanks that he is part of our lives.

Second, we are here to grieve.

As Christians, we feel mixed emotions at death: joy and sorrow. We grieve the dead because we miss them. We liked being with them, and there is a hole in our lives now that they are gone.

I'll miss so many things about Ran, but most of all, I'll miss his laugh. No one laughed like that. It was an uproarious laugh, almost a cackle. And he laughed so often. Ran and my father and friends like Walter Lee loved jokes, but they loved the same jokes over and over again. The more they told them, the sooner they laughed.

So there is a hole in our hearts where that laughter used to be, but that hole is also where we find the compassion of God.

So, let us remember it's okay to grieve: To let the tears run down our faces. For they are the waters of baptism that wash our hearts clean.

To celebrate, to grieve, and to give thanks to God.

We give thanks because, as Paul says, *"Neither death, nor life . . . will . . . separate us from the love of God in Christ Jesus our Lord."* Amid our tears we know that God's love is stronger than death.

We had a funeral in my church a month or so ago, and afterwards a child asked me: "So what does heaven look like anyway?"

I stalled and said back, "Well, what do you think?"

She thought a minute and then said: "Oh, I think it's a big playground."

Well, maybe it is, but on this day I have a different image: Maybe heaven's a large house set back from the street. It could be any address, but it happens to be 87 Furman Avenue, Asheville, North Carolina. The house has a porch where men and women rock back and forth, telling stories of who is related to whom. On that porch the saints laugh and talk and drink and enjoy abundant life. And they are all there: There's Sadie and Martha and Matilda and Edith and Richard, and now Ransom.

That's why, amid our sorrow, we give thanks. For today Ran is part of the company of heaven.

He is with our Lord in Paradise. He, too, is one of the saints. And for that we say, "Alleluia! Alleluia! Alleluia!"

The Ministry of Friendship
Celebration of a New Ministry

 EPHESIANS 4:7, 11–16; JOHN 15:9–16

Big decisions are never simple. Even when we think they are over, they aren't over. Remember buying a house? Remember deciding to get married? Or, more to the point, remember when St. Andrew's decided to call Susan Gaumer as its rector?

When we finally make a big decision, we are filled with relief and excitement:

> *Thank God, the search is over.*
> *Now we can stop living in limbo.*
> *Now we can give Susan all that work that we don't want to do.*
> *Now we can go back to being ordinary lay folks and let her do*
> *the priestly stuff.*

First, relief and then excitement for the future, because we are certain that the future will conform to our vision of what it ought to be. At some point, and usually this is around three o'clock in the morning, the euphoria wears off and we ask ourselves: *What have we gotten ourselves into?* We know our life together is going to change, but how? We know we've been *called* but we wonder, *called to what?*

Tonight we are here to celebrate the beginning of new ministry, but whose ministry are we celebrating? Is it just about Susan Gaumer? Is this some kind of coronation, or is God calling this whole parish to a new ministry? And if so, to what?

We have been talking about the ministry of all baptized persons, but we so seldom act upon it. Jesus is speaking to his disciples and telling them:

I do not call you servants any longer, because the servant does not
know what the master is doing, but I have called you friends.

Friends. Friends, not laity, not clergy, not even champions for some
wonderful cause, or self-righteous people who know everything, but
friends.

Maybe that's a surprise. Maybe it's like discovering the house you
bought has doors that don't shut, or the spouse you married suddenly
doesn't hang on every pearl of wisdom from your mouth. Or that this
ministry you thought you called Susan Gaumer for is not what you bar-
gained for. Maybe you were thinking the ministry of St. Andrew's was
just to be happy or successful or properly Episcopalian.

But we are called to be part of this ministry of friendship. Well,
what does that mean?

First—friends are loyal. They are connected to one another. There
is a bond that exists between friends. We think of the Musketeers thing
of "one for all and all for one." But it's true. Friends stand up for you.
Whenever I feel blue, whenever my ego is in sore need of repair, I call
one of my friends. I don't usually ask for advice. We just talk and I feel
better. I know that someone is for me. I know that someone appreciates
me just for being me.

When I call up Susie and ask her advice, I confess I really don't care
what she says. I'm not writing it down. I just want to hear her voice. I
want to know that through her I am connected to the love of Jesus
Christ and I am part of the body.

Jesus calls us to be friends. Friends walk with one another wherever the journey leads. Friends are willing to suffer with one another.

When I was in Nashville, a young boy there contracted leukemia.
He had to take chemotherapy, and as a result, his hair fell out. Now the
boy, Samuel, was scared about going back to his third grade class. He
didn't want to look different. He didn't want to feel different. But when
he walked into his room, he saw that all the boys had shaved their heads,
too.

The ministry of friendship is discovering Christ in the midst of us.
Susie's job as rector is not to rule the roost, not to perform dazzling
sacramental acts that amaze an audience, but to walk with you and teach
you how to walk together as friends.

Second, friendship is not exclusive like romantic love, but is inclusive. My love for my wife and my children is exclusive. I cannot love another woman or child in the way I love them, but friendship is different. Yes, my kids have all sorts of conversations about "best friends," but that isn't friendship in its purest form.

The word *companion* means *together at bread*. Our image of friends is the table at which we all are together with our Lord. The closer we are to him, the closer we are to each other and vice versa. "*I have called you friends,*" Jesus says, because he wants us to grow in love: in our love for him, our love for one another, and our love for those we don't yet know. Having friends enables you to make friends, because you know what friendship is. My guess is that just as you have welcomed Susan and Dick and Cricket and Matt, so you are called to welcome in the stranger who will come to your door in the years to come. *I have called you to be friends* means that you are saving a seat at the table for all those friends you have yet to meet, because as you greet them, you greet our Lord.

So friendship is being loyal; friendship is inclusive; and third, friendship is joyous.

C. S. Lewis says:

> Friendship is unnecessary, like philosophy, like art, like the universe itself (for God did not need to create). It has no survival value; rather it is one of those things which give value to survival.[13]

It's like going to a restaurant. You could eat by yourself, but who wants to? Friends are part of what gives our world color. Our friends are our missing parts. They bring out parts of ourselves that would remain hidden otherwise. Friends are what keep us from worshipping ourselves. They remind us that the mystery of Christ is bigger than any one of us.

So St. Andrew's, like every parish, is called to seek out those who are different, those with whom we disagree, those who don't think they belong, and to call them here as friends. Jesus came that we might have life more abundantly, and surely one way is through friendship.

---

13. C. S. Lewis, *The Four Loves* (New York: Harcourt Brace Jovanovich, 1960), 103.

There's a legend about Judas after the crucifixion that is too good not to be true. After Calvary, Judas fell into a bottomless, dark pit and lay there alone. He lay there for years and years in complete despair. But one day he lifted his head and looked up. At the top of the pit he saw a thin shaft of light so dim he wasn't really sure it was there. So he began the long climb to the top.

For months and months he climbed. And when he had almost given up, he came to the ledge. Pulling himself up, he found himself in a small, upper room somewhere in Jerusalem. There was a table with bread and wine. Seated there were a group of people listening to a young rabbi. As Judas looked, the rabbi said:

> *Judas, friend. You are here at last. We couldn't start without you. Come, join us.*

I have called you friends.

In the midst of this complex life, Jesus is calling this parish to embrace this ministry of friendship, to suffer with one another, to be joyous. And to reach out to those who feel as if they have fallen into a dark pit. And to say to them: *Welcome, we are saving you a seat because you are a friend.*

Remembering Our Ministry

An Ordination Sermon

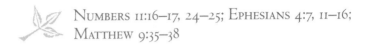 NUMBERS 11:16–17, 24–25; EPHESIANS 4:7, 11–16; MATTHEW 9:35–38

When I told my mother that I had been asked to preach at this ordination, she said, *"Won't that be fun? Everyone will be all gussied up!"* And, looking around, I guess they are. These feasts days are what we do best: magnificent music—gorgeous sanctuary—and in a moment these eight soon-to-be priests will don elegant stoles and chasubles. Ordinations are days to get gussied up.

I don't want to play Scrooge here, but I cannot assure the eight of you that you are on the verge of a career of bliss, either. The danger of getting gussied up is that we pretend that everything you do will involve all this magnificent finery. So amid all our celebration, let's don't lose sight of what's ahead. Which brings me to the reading from Numbers. Isn't it interesting to see what the framers of the lectionary have done with this reading?

Talk about dressing things up! We heard God tell Moses to gather seventy of the elders in the tent of meeting so that God can spread some of the spirit of Moses on these people and so they will then prophesy.

Now that's a picture of the church suitable for ordination. The eight of you can imagine yourselves walking into a vestry meeting and magnanimously bestowing some of the Spirit given to you today upon those adoring and eternally appreciative men and women. Then you can send them off into the world to prophesy in places a safe distance away from the parish. It's a nice picture: a sort of a Palestinian version of George Hebert's *The Country Parson*. But it leaves too much out.

To paint this picture, we skip from verse 18 to 24 and we don't get the preamble, either. What is it that got left out?

First of all, the reason Moses talks to God is that the people are driving him crazy. They are murmuring again:

> *If only we had meat to eat! We remember the fish we used to eat in Egypt . . . the cucumbers, the melons, the leeks.*

I confess I have never had anyone get angry at me because my explanation of the Trinity is inadequate. No one has ever called the bishop and said, *"Porter's Christology is slightly askew."* But when I shortened the coffee hour to increase our Christian education time, the people of St. Gregory's did more than murmur.

To make it worse for Moses, he catches it from both sides. We also left out this verse: *Then the Lord became very angry.* So Moses does what we'd all like to do. He screams back:

> *Why have you treated [me] so badly? . . . Did I conceive all this people? . . . I am not able to carry all this people alone, for they are too heavy for me. If this is the way you are going to treat me, put me to death at once.*

The people are screaming at Moses, and Moses is screaming at God, and God is screaming back.

No wonder we skipped over that part. Is there any good reason to bring it up? This makes it seem as if the church has taken the fun out of the dysfunctional. Should we ignore this and pretend that your life as a priest will be out of one of Jan Karon's novels?

Well, no. Instead, let's see what the story says about your ministry—about real ministry.

First, if nothing else, the story says that ministry is always a three-way conversation. Admittedly in this case it's a heated conversation, but Moses knows that he has no idea what to do. So he loudly—rather assertively—talks to God.

Ce Ce and Sean, it may be disappointing, but your people are not interested in how smart you are. They want to know what you have to say about life's primal elements: birth and death; joy and pain. They want to know what you have to say about being lost in the only desert, about feeling a million miles from home. They want to know what to do when they are sick and tired of being sick and tired. They want to know if you can talk to God, because they want *you* to remind them that there is a God to talk to.

So often we think our job is to be the wizard of Oz: the person putting on a big show. But our job is more like being the scarecrow: someone who has been on the cross and is not afraid to walk with all those who are trying to get home.

Sometimes clergy and laity and God scream at each other. Sometimes we cry with each other, and a lot of the time we laugh with each other, but you are to keep the conversation going.

Perhaps the second piece of good news is this: ministry is not about performing; it's about equipping the saints for ministry. God does not tell Moses: learn to delegate; God tells Moses, "I will share some of your Spirit with your people."

Wouldn't it be wonderful if we could just hand out lists of jobs that we don't want to do and tell people, "I am empowering you for ministry—go handle stewardship." But our task is deeper and more inti-mate than that. The grace you receive today is to be shared. It is to be spread among your people. We only dare to take on this task because God's love is so strong and so abundant that if we only get out of the way it will come out of us. It will spread.

Notice that the seventy don't feed anyone. God does that. Moses has asked for help with food and God gives seventy people to help him, but it's not with the food. No, God spreads the Spirit and the people prophesy. They see their lives and the world in a new way.

One of my friends, Frank, has a dear friend who is dying of an incurable disease. Her name is Helen. A few months ago, Helen was feeling as if she was wandering in the desert. She felt as if she had only mealy bread to eat, and the promised land was a long way away. She complained to Frank, and he wanted to help, but he couldn't cure her. Then he remembered that his godmother had gone to Japan and had bought a pure silk kimono. Upon her death she had given this to Frank. So he took the kimono and went to Helen's house and told her:

*When you feel alone and hopeless, put this on and remember that
I love you.*

The spirit of God spreads, so your job—Mark, Thomas, and Gay—is to pollinate the world with that Spirit. People don't want jobs to do. They want grace. People don't come to keep the church machine going, they come to share in the vision of the kingdom of God. You are the ones who will distribute the bread of life and the cup of salvation. When you give them these, give them part of your life of Spirit. Let these new chasubles be silk kimonos so that they remind all the Helens in your churches how much God loves them and spread that love in the world.

Finally, the good news is that the pattern of the world is death and resurrection. God spreads the Spirit on the seventy, but do you think that stops them from complaining? A few verses later someone complains that Eldad and Medad are prophesying. Then the people whine about going into Canaan because their warriors are too fierce, and on and on.

Our problems never go away. Whatever we do, our world is always going to be broken. But the peace of God, which surpasses all understanding, doesn't come from any confidence in our ability to manage this mess because it will not be managed. Instead—Patty, Beth, and Carolynne—God in Christ through the Holy Spirit is inviting you and all God's people into the Way.

We are always dying; we are always rising. That finally is the mystery of faith, yet how hard it is for us to grasp. We keep thinking that our job is to get the people better food, nicer churches, bigger programs, so we will have more impressive resumes. No, our job is to invite all men and women into the mystery of rising and dying with Christ.

Ce Ce, Sean, Thomas, Mark, Gay, Patty, Beth, and Carolynne:

On this day of your ordination to the priesthood, on this day where we are all gussied up, remember that when your people and yourself want some cucumbers and meat, your task is to keep the conversation going; to talk and listen to God and to talk and listen to the people.

Remember not to give out jobs but to spread the Spirit God gives you; and remember that we offer not solutions to problems but a life of death and resurrection.

If you remember these things, then throughout your days as priests in Christ's Church, the peace of God, which surpasses all understanding, will guard your hearts and your minds in Christ Jesus.